FRIENDS
OF ACPL

W9-AXI-206

DATING FOR
YOUNG CATHOLICS

DATING FOR
YOUNG CATHOLICS

Very Rev. Msgr. George A. Kelly

Doubleday & Company, Inc.
Garden City, New York
1963

301.1584
K296d

168

79 10422 1

Nihil obstat: Daniel V. Flynn, J.C.D.
                  Censor Librorum

Imprimatur: ✠ Francis Cardinal Spellman
                  Archbishop of New York

                  December 5, 1962

The *nihil obstat* and *imprimatur* are official declarations
that a book or pamphlet is free of doctrinal or moral error.
No implication is contained therein that those who have
granted the *nihil obstat* and *imprimatur* agree with the
contents, opinions, or statements expressed.

Library of Congress Catalog Card Number 63–8754
Copyright © 1961, 1962, 1963 by George A. Kelly
All Rights Reserved
Printed in the United States of America
First Edition

1209379

CONTENTS

AUTHOR'S PREFACE

Dating for Young Catholics is written for teen-agers, to be read by them.

This book grew out of a series of thirty-two articles written in 1961 for *Hi-Time Magazine,* that popular Catholic publication read weekly by thousands of high school students across the country.

The favorable response by priests, teaching sisters and brothers, boys and girls themselves, to these articles has encouraged the writer to think that in book form the subject matter here treated will contribute in some small way to the better education of Catholic youth still somewhat removed by time from that serious commitment usually called "engagement."

In many ways, *Dating for Young Catholics* can be classified under the heading "remote preparation for marriage," a particularly urgent form of education for Catholics in our day and in our country, and one occasionally neglected by those more preoccupied with the pressing problems of bad marriages, divorce, contraception, illegitimacy and juvenile crime.

While a great deal of effort has gone into preparing engaged couples for marriage through pre-Cana Conferences (and with astounding success), education for courtship has lagged somewhat behind. Perhaps this is due to the fact that teen-agers are not a ready-made audience like engaged couples. Furthermore, fifteen-, sixteen-, even seventeen-year-olds are enjoying themselves too much outside of school hours to want to be reminded at night or on weekends of serious subjects. Finally, not all Catholic specialists in the field of family-life education agree on the subject matter of "remote preparation for marriage." Yet in spite of these obstacles we may be missing a never-to-be-recovered opportunity.

By the time the engaged couple comes to pre-Cana, the die might well be cast. The young man and woman might already be mismated. Certain habits of mind and morals might now be fixed. Because they have become serious and have already mutually agreed on a variety of subjects relating to married life, the short time spent at a pre-Cana series might not be enough to insure a Christian way of life after the wedding day.

But the uncommitted teen-ager is a different breed. He is struggling for good ideas. He is looking for the best. And being really free, he can more objectively think through such controversial matters as going steady, early marriage, chastity, the qualifications of a good future spouse, mixed marriage, contraception, divorce, the working wife and a host of other matters that demand positive and Christian thinking by potential husbands and wives.

If pre-Cana may be too late, then, early courtship may be the right time for effective education. Parents, parish priests, religious teachers in Catholic high schools, directors of Confraternity classes are beginning to realize this. And to help them accomplish their objectives, this book was written, not only to be put into the hands of Catholic youth under their care, but as a tool for classroom or parish discussion on a variety of topics of lively interest to the adolescent. Planned discussions of this kind are popular and give the young a chance, under the guidance of a trained leader, to raise questions, resolve doubts and appreciate the beauty of Catholic ideals, while giving them support in their struggles against the secular forces that threaten to engulf them.

For contributions to the successful publication of this book, my special thanks to Miss Henriette Mackin, managing editor of *Hi-Time Magazine,* Mr. John J. Delaney of Doubleday and Company, and to Mr. John Springer, member of the Advisory Board of the Family Life Bureau, Archdiocese of New York.

GEORGE A. KELLY

1. WHEN YOU DATE, YOU ARE PREPARING FOR MARRIAGE

A wise professor often remarked that few adults could remember when they first began to date and that even husbands and wives often couldn't recall when they had their first date together. "Yet these days are two of the most important of your life," he used to say.

This teacher was quite right. When you begin to date, you begin a new way of life. Probably for the first time, you begin to realize what makes boys and girls so different in an emotional and intellectual as well as a physical way. You begin to think of the opposite sex more distinctly as men or women. You begin to look forward to when you yourself will be a husband or wife—a fully matured adult.

At age fourteen or so, it may seem farfetched to ask you to think of dating as a step toward marriage. But it will seem less farfetched with every passing year. By the time you are nineteen or twenty, the idea of marriage may be very much in the forefront when you date. It's a fact that one or more graduates of almost every high school in the country marches up the aisle soon after graduation every year.

Many societies in Asia and Europe are more realistic about dating than we are. There, the people know that it's basically the differences between the sexes that bring a boy and girl together. They realize that only in marriage can the desire for the opposite sex be morally exercised. So when youngsters there begin to date, they have one major intention—to marry.

A little thought will convince you that dating is a step toward marriage. It's obvious that when the average boy and girl first see each other, they don't immediately decide that they're in love and that no one else will do. Maybe "love at first sight" is the usual routine in the movies, but it rarely occurs in real life.

What generally happens is that the boy and girl are mildly attracted to each other. They date, have a good time, and discover that they'd like to date again. After a while, they go steady. And finally they decide to share their lives together.

In cases like this, love develops gradually. No bells ring and no lightning strikes and no newspaper headlines the news on page one.

What does this prove? Two things:

1. You never know, once you begin to date a certain person, whether you will be joining him or her at the altar some fine day in the future. This much I also know: You don't get married in our society without dating. Every time you date, therefore, there is some possibility that your partner on the date will wind up as your partner in marriage.

2. Once you begin to date the same individual regularly, you increase the likelihood of marriage. Nobody has exact figures to show how many persons the average husband and wife dated before they met their marriage partner. But I'd guess that the average boy or girl does not regularly date more than three or four persons before meeting the one who will be his or hers for life.

This adds up to the fact that you ought to date only those you wouldn't be ashamed to marry. Of course, someone who may seem to be a charmer at a distance may turn out to be a creep on a date. But at least when you made the date, you didn't know the whole story. You didn't make it knowing full well that you'd never want to sign up the particular boy or girl on a long-term contract.

This point is important because, as the poets keep telling us, "love is blind." A boy may be conceited, selfish, unwilling or unable to accept responsibility—somebody who thinks only of his own comfort. But the girl who falls in love with him overlooks all those defects which stick out like a sore thumb to everyone else. A girl may spend hours before a mirror every day, admiring herself, and may expect to be waited on hand and foot. But he too is blind to those faults that would make her a horror to live with.

Keeping in mind that dating is a preparation for marriage, can actually increase your enjoyment of it. With this knowledge, you will be able to see a purpose in everything you do. Suppose your date does turn out to be a fizzle. You can still learn something worthwhile, as did one teen-ager I know. He came home from a dance and made a puzzling remark. "I had a terrible time, but I'm glad I went," he said. "My date didn't stop yakking from the second I met her until I took her home. I'm positive now that that's one type I never want to marry."

In order to date constructively, you should have an idea of what marriage is all about. Why do people marry, anyway? Why is marriage a sacrament? Why does the Church teach that you must stay married for life? What kind of people make the best marriage partners? If you get the answers to these questions now, you'll have some idea of the rights and duties of the married state. Then you'll be able to choose your dating partners with care and then you'll also assure yourself of getting the kind of lifetime partner that you want.

I'll try to answer these questions in the chapters to follow. I'll show you why Catholic marriage should be regarded as a vocation in which you do an important work for God, and I'll outline exactly what God and the Church teach us about this work you'll take on when you utter those fateful words, "I do."

Once we understand the nature of marriage, we'll be able to consider the steps in dating leading up to it. I'll give you down-to-earth facts about the qualities that can make you more attractive to the opposite sex. I'll answer questions I am often asked about necking, etc., and I'll try to explain the difference between a passing crush and real love—the kind that not only will last but will actually grow richer with the years.

I'll try to show you how to date more effectively. And

since dating is just preparing for marriage, my real purpose
is to show you what you can do now to have a more successful marriage when you take that great plunge.

This is a mighty important subject. Because if you make a
successful marriage, you assure yourself not only of the greatest possible measure of happiness here on earth, but also of
your eternal salvation in heaven.

2. UNDERSTAND YOURSELF FIRST!

Some of the most famous words in all the world were written by William Shakespeare for his play *Hamlet*. The scene is Denmark. An old father, Polonius, is giving some advice to his son Laertes who is leaving for France:

"This above all: to thine own self be true, And it must follow, as the night the day, Thou canst not then be false to any man."

This is excellent advice for today, for tomorrow and for life. It is important in your dating, and most important of all in your selection of a marriage partner.

To put Shakespeare's advice into practice, you must first understand yourself. For if you are to be true to yourself, you must first know who you are, why you were born, where you are going. Much of the confusion and lack of purpose shown by old and young results from their failure to understand exactly what they're supposed to be doing in life.

Fundamental, you say? Of course. But only by starting with fundamentals can we answer many of our most important questions.

For instance, who are you? You know you are a creature composed of body and soul and made in the image and likeness of God. You know that your body may often be in conflict with your soul—that the instincts of your flesh may war against the true aims of your spirit.

You also know that in this war, your soul must triumph over your body. You know it, because your final goal is union with God. You were made "to know Him, to love Him and to serve Him in this world in order to be happy with Him forever in the next."

So it will help you to know about the weaknesses we all have and must overcome in order to achieve our salvation.

You should also know about the strengths and weaknesses you yourself possess to a greater or lesser degree than boys and girls you know.

About the weaknesses of all of us: Even the wisest of men have great limitations. None of us has the experience and wisdom to know everything that is good for us. Saints have sometimes wondered why certain suffering was necessary; they didn't know what was in the mind of God. All of us must accept the rules laid down by our Creator, because nobody is so wise that he can achieve his salvation without God's help.

We must depend on God for many reasons, of course, one of them being that nobody knows what lies ahead. For example, a high school freshman has only a vague idea of the problems he'll face as a married man. If he won't listen to someone who knows more about the subject, he'll make plenty of serious mistakes. Even a seventy-five-year-old doesn't know what problems lie ahead for him, or of the experience that comes when he draws his last breath. All our lives we need someone to tell us what we must do. That Someone is God, speaking through His Church.

Why We Call Her "Mother Church"

There's a good reason why we speak about "Mother Church." Like any mother, she knows a great deal more than her children do. And like your own mother, she has received a responsibility from God to look after you. It's her job to tell you what you must do to be saved. She always has your best interests at heart—and unless you listen to her, sometime you might find yourself in real spiritual trouble.

For a minute, consider the problems of a mother of a four-year-old child. You'd certainly agree that she has to tell the child what to do. If she saw him playing with a sharp knife, she'd have to take it from him—maybe even paddle his bottom if he kept playing with it after she told him to stop. The boy might wail and toss a tantrum because in his small mind there's nothing wrong with a knife. It's even a lot of fun, when you see how it makes little notches in the furniture.

He doesn't have the experience to know that the knife could cause hundreds of dollars' worth of destruction, could result in serious injury to him or the loss of his life. A few years from now, he may know better. But he doesn't know it today. He's got to take his mother's word for it.

Wouldn't you say that she had the obligation to take the knife away—in fact, that she had the duty to keep him from hurting himself? The child hasn't been alive long enough to realize all the harm that could be done from something he thinks is great fun.

A little child doesn't know all the good that can result from good habits, either. So he has to take it on his mother's say-so that drinking milk will give him a strong body, good bones, good teeth. That a good night's sleep is necessary to help him grow properly, to have good nerves, to be alive and alert during the day. And so on.

He does what she tells him because, first of all, he trusts her. He knows that his mother knows best. But suppose you met a four- or five-year-old who had decided that he knew more than his mother did, that he could make up his mind about what foods to eat, how much sleep to get, what sort of other youngsters he played with. If you saw a brat like that, you'd probably say that the mother wasn't doing her job—that the first thing she should do would be to let him know who was boss.

We were all model kids, of course. But when we get a little older, we sometimes think we know more than does Mother Church. Maybe we think, for instance, that we're old enough to play with things that are just as dangerous for us at sixteen as matches are dangerous for the lad of six. This is one mistake we must avoid, however, if we want to get the best out of life. Because just as a human mother has her children's best interests at heart, so too does the Church have our welfare in the forefront of her mind. And we shouldn't forget that she knows what she's talking about, because she has had thousands of years of experience.

Suppose you asked the mother of ten children how she raised them. She'd probably tell you she did a better job on the last than on Number One. That's natural. By the time Number Ten arrived, she had had the opportunity to see, first hand, what mistakes she may have made with the earlier ones. By then, she knew from her actual experience which methods work and which ones don't. Maybe when her first child was a high school sophomore, she let him stay out late during school nights. She had a chance to see how this running around had a bad effect on his marks in school—maybe even on his health. So when the second or third child reached high school age, she set limits on hours out and insisted that he be in bed at a certain time.

Well, if someone with ten children can qualify as an experienced mother, how about one with ten million times ten? The Church has been watching over the growth of her spiritual children for almost two thousand years now, and she's had a better chance than any other body in the world to observe what things lead to a person's spiritual betterment—and what things lead to harm.

If you want a quick rule to success in your life, therefore, it's this: Do what Mother Church tells you. She has seen millions upon millions of her children grow up, begin dating, get married, have children, become grandparents—go through the whole routine of living. She has the road map of life. She knows where the pitfalls are. She knows where some people get off the road and lose their way. She knows how to avoid the detours. If you follow the route she has laid out, you'll be sure of reaching your goal of heaven.

One thing you must keep in mind, however. Mother Church, when she lays out the route for us to follow, does not act solely on her own initiative. Nor do her guidelines originate merely from her long experience. Rather is she the builder for the Divine Architect who is God. It is God who has said much about how we should live. It is Christ who told the Twelve Apostles to teach "all things whatsoever I have commanded you." Basically, then, when we speak of "morals" we are not talking about man-made rules, but God-inspired directions.

We Don't Vote on Morality

A strange idea has popped up in recent years that suggests that we can decide moral questions on a vote basis. According to this notion, if 51 percent of a group decide that necking is okay to a point just short of intercourse, then such necking should be permitted. This idea operates on the belief that all life is a democracy—that the majority vote should prevail. Nothing could be further than the truth.

We live in a world in which the rules are made for us by God, Our Creator. We can vote every day of our lives and still not change those rules. For instance, He has decreed that all men must die. Even if all mankind voted 100 percent to change that situation, we'd continue to die.

God created the law of gravity. We could vote to abolish it —but we'd still plunge to death if we decided to step off the Empire State Building. A majority of voters can elect a president or prime minister, but suppose a majority voted to eliminate the effect of poison on the human body. The next person who drank the poison would die as usual.

The important thing to understand about ourselves, therefore, is that God created the conditions under which we must live. No matter what our physical instincts might say, or what temptations come to us, we must do certain things His way. In other words, we must obey His Commandments.

It is also well to realize that you have a distinct personality, and therefore will see life somewhat differently from those about you. The influence of your parents and of other adults who have helped in your upbringing will play an important part in how you react to certain circumstances. In addition, the nature God has given you is a big factor.

As you know, some of us tend to be high-strung while others by nature are relaxed and easygoing. Some of us are sensitive; others, tough-skinned. One boy may seem to be honest by nature. Another may find that it's not difficult to resist thoughts of impurities. A third may have no trouble with disobedience whereas his own brother gets into hot water because he won't do what's expected of him.

If you doubt that you have a distinct personality, just watch your class studying for an exam. The class "brain" will take ten minutes to learn everything that needs to be known. Another will struggle over the material for an hour and won't know it.

It's true, of course, that none of us knows himself perfectly. But we can tell, in a general way, what our strengths and weaknesses are. We certainly know, for example, if we fly off the handle more readily than the next person. If we stop to think about it, we can tell whether we're bossy or easygoing—whether we always want our own way, or generally will do things as the next person wants them done. We know whether we're willing to accept an adult's advice about our conduct, or whether we must do things our way and learn in the hardest manner possible. We can tell whether we're the affectionate type and find it easy to say kind words to parents, friends, relatives, or whether we freeze up inside when the situation calls for a little affection.

Knowing these things about yourselves, you can figure out your own strong and weak points. You'll know what sort of partner you should look for—one who'll help you retain your strengths, and who'll also help you get rid of your weaknesses.

Ever notice an older couple married twenty-five years or so? You might have seen that their mannerisms were generally quite similar. What has happened is that they have combined their strengths and weaknesses to some extent and have developed a kind of joint personality. The man who once was inclined to be impetuous may have taken on some of the relaxed, let's-think-it-over qualities of his wife. The young bride who was inclined to be a scatterbrain may have learned to think more logically as she grew older. The young man who thought anything was permissible as long as it made a buck, may have come under the influence of his wiser wife and now realizes that there are higher values than mere money-making.

To sum up: If you want to date successfully—and therefore to marry successfully—you should try to understand yourself. Understand what your weaknesses are and look for someone who'll help you overcome them. Then your relationship with this other person will be an uplifting one—one that will help you achieve the purpose for which you were born.

3. THE NATURE OF THE SEXES

You may have heard about the time a debate was raging in the French Chamber of Deputies. One of the members of the Assembly arose and began to discuss the necessity of setting up different working conditions for women from those established for men. "It is a fact," he stated pompously, "there is a great difference between the sexes."

At that point, a voice in the gallery responded, "Long live the difference."

Everyone aged two or over probably realizes that there are physical distinctions between males and females. What many people don't realize is that there are other differences as well—differences that go far beyond mere physical characteristics.

Imagine two women are standing at a store counter. They get into an argument over which should be served first. Suddenly one woman stands back, doubles her fist and wallops the other on the chin. You'd be astonished at the sight. Why? Because her action is unladylike—foreign, you might say, to the nature of a woman.

Or suppose two men are arguing. Instead of giving vent to their feelings by yelling or punching each other, they both go off to different corners and begin to cry. You'd be amazed, perhaps even nauseated. Why? Again, because they're not doing a "manly" thing.

I could spend hours enumerating differences between men and women—differences in how they think and act, in their emotional responses to the things they see, in the way that they view life. Let me cite a few:

By nature, a man tends to be decisive, and once he makes up his mind, he's likely to think of it as final. But after a woman's decision is seemingly set, she may change it and decide upon another course. Hence, woman's prerogative to "change her mind."

In considering a problem, a woman will be more inclined to trust her intuition than her sense of logic. On the other hand, her husband will be "logical." He'll try to argue from what he thinks are the facts—not from how he feels about them.

A man tends to be direct and straightforward. His wife usually is less likely to accept things at their face value. She may say one thing, feeling that she is making her real meaning perfectly plain. Because that's her nature, she may find herself thinking her husband means something other than what he says.

A man is often gruff. He tends to hide his emotions. A woman is more likely to be emotional—to cry more easily, to show it when her feelings are hurt.

There's been a tendency in recent times to minimize differences between men and women. For example, women hold many jobs that used to be the prerogative of men exclusively. There are women doctors, women lawyers, women scientists, women cab drivers, and so on. At the same time, you can see men doing things around the house which used to be done entirely by women. You see them washing dishes, doing housework, shopping for groceries, changing baby's diapers, and so on. To some extent, this is fine. Good riddance to those days when the man was the Lord and Master and his wife was little more than a slave who had to do his bidding.

But don't make the mistake of thinking that real fundamental differences between men and women don't exist and won't exist until the end of time. For example, don't hold your breath until you see a boxing match on television in which a woman heavyweight steps into the ring to challenge the male champ of the world. Why won't you ever see such a thing? Because such a match would violate all the instincts of mankind. The woman has not been made for such a contest. And the man who allowed himself to enter the ring under such circumstances would violate our fundamental instincts by fighting someone who is physically weaker by nature.

Why Are Men and Women Different?

Such differences exist because of the different roles which God has given men and women to play.

The Creator planned that man should be the head and woman the heart of the family. In setting up patterns for the conception, birth and education of children, He arranged that a child should have personal care for a long period of years, until he grew strong enough and smart enough to care for himself. In His wisdom, He gave woman the emotional qualities to enable her to love and educate her young ones. That's why woman is "soft." Her nature is ideally suited to the care and education of the young.

While a mother cares for her child, someone must provide for both of them. That person is the husband and father. And he has the qualities to play his role more efficiently. He is generally stronger physically, with quicker reflexes—an asset important today as well as when his main job was to fish and hunt. He generally has a greater ability to withstand the emotional strain of providing for a family in a competitive world.

There are usually two sides, at least, to the typical characteristics of the sexes. This condition is like a "two-for-one" sale in which you buy one item and get another free. In this case, you get a personality characteristic you want but along with it, you'll have to take some aspects of it you don't like.

Example: A typical man takes charge of a situation with determination and he will get things done. Good! But that personality characteristic which serves him very well at work does not change suddenly when he comes home. Because of his nature, he is impatient with family members who don't act as decisively as he does.

By nature, his wife is gentle, soft. She's more ready to perform a kindness for someone else. The other side of this quality is that she's inclined to be an "easy mark." Her husband must be thankful for the loving quality, but also must accept the fact that at times people will seem to be taking advantage of her.

Remember this important fact: God made men and women differently because He expects them to do different jobs. The sexes are complementary: The typical male qualities, when added to those of the female, produce a oneness that is stronger than either the male or female separately.

When you begin to date, therefore, don't expect to find somebody like the person you see in the mirror every day. That is why I stressed earlier that you should understand yourself first. Because if you realize what kind of personality you have and can honestly recognize your weak and strong points, you may realize how someone of the opposite sex might help you to overcome your defects by providing strong supports where you are weak.

Also remember, however, that the sexes are alike in certain fundamental things. Foremost, of course, men and women are alike in having souls which must be protected and saved. They are also similar in that they possess intellect and heart.

A man and woman might be compared to a table and chair. Both are made of wood, which has identical qualities. But their shapes are different, and they have different functions to perform.

You could eat dinner while sitting on a chair without the table, or while standing at the table without the chair. But it's obviously better to use both at the same time. A dining room would be a mighty silly place with two tables and no chairs, or with two chairs and no table.

Just as a table has been made in order to perform one function and the chair has been designed for another, so too do man and woman have different purposes. Together, they make a team.

4. DON'T BE IMPATIENT TO DATE!

It was a sunny June day not so long ago when John Jones, nineteen, stood before the priest at the altar and promised to love, honor, and cherish Mary Smith, eighteen, until death. They had a wedding reception and went off on a honeymoon to Niagara Falls.

Two years later, they came to the conclusion that they couldn't stand each other. Mary went home to her parents and John went seven hundred miles away and found a job in Chicago. To the best of his wife's knowledge, he now lives in a flea-ridden furnished room and can be found almost any night in a crummy bar.

What went wrong with these two? People who knew John and Mary (not their real names, of course) vouch that both were good kids with good hearts. Both could have become responsible adults and could have made a successful marriage—*if* they had waited until they were mature enough before they took on the responsibilities of husband and wife.

If you want to find the real source of trouble in their marriage, I think you could blame the fact that they married too early. And they married too early because they went steady too early. They were caught up in the popular but false idea that members of the opposite sexes can go together and be "good friends" year after year.

They did not realize that boys and girls who associate together are preparing for marriage. If they date a great deal in their early teens, they're probably going too fast in that direction. They are likely to reach the destination—marriage—before they are ready to accept all its duties.

It was like that with John and Mary. John had only the vaguest notion of what would be expected of him. While he knew that he should provide for his family, he had no clear idea of how many sacrifices he would have to make to keep himself, his wife and their children adequately fed, housed and clothed. And he had only the vaguest notion of the number of compromises required to live together with another human being—habits he would have to change, little luxuries he would have to give up, considerate gestures he continually would have to make.

For her part, his bride lived in a dream world where "love conquers all." She believed that a wife and mother somehow can get her work done without any real effort.

There's Wisdom in Waiting

As you may have gathered by now, my purpose in this chapter is to point out why it's wise to wait awhile before you date—and why your life won't be ruined if you don't go steady while you're in high school. In fact, most high school boys and girls don't date regularly, so you needn't feel you're destined to lead a life of single bliss just because you don't have a boy friend or girl friend at this stage in your life.

A statistician once figured out that the average period between a person's first date and marriage is about six years. According to this, a girl or boy who began dating at twelve is more likely to marry at eighteen than one who began at fifteen or so. Begin dating at fifteen, these figures indicate, and marriage at around twenty-one would be an average result. Start dating at eighteen and your march up the altar might take place at around twenty-four.

Many reasons could be cited to explain why this average period is what it is. For instance, when most boys and girls begin to date, they get a great deal of satisfaction out of the idea of dating. After a while, though, they expect more from their partner—companionship, sense of humor, and so on. And after that, as they come to know the opposite sex better, they start thinking about other qualities they would like their dates to have. Gradually, they progress to where they want their date to have all the qualities they'd like in a husband or wife.

The continued association with the opposite sex also builds up strong physical desires. This could hardly be otherwise, since the urge that God implanted is so strong. Much of the feeling of love that a young man has for a young woman, and vice versa, can be expressed adequately only in a physical relationship. As you know, the sexual expression of love outside of marriage is a sin. In order to express their feelings for each other in a lawful way, the thoughts of the young man and woman naturally turn to marriage.

So the age when dating begins has a lot to do with the age when the marriage chimes are sounded. Early dating, therefore, is more likely to lead to early marriage—and an early marriage is less likely to succeed than one between a man and woman old enough to understand fully what they're getting into.

Somebody once said that there are statistics for everything. We certainly have plenty about divorce. And they prove that the proportion of broken marriages is far greater among those who marry in their teens than it is among those who are older than twenty-one when they marry. Not only do marriages of twenty-year-olds have less chance to last. It's also more likely that in the marriages that do last, the husband and wife will have a rougher time learning to get along together.

It's strange that more and more youngsters are marrying before they're old enough to know what life is all about, because the problems of marriage today are probably more complicated than they've ever been.

You'll Need All the Education You Can Get

Take just one thing—the demand for well-educated men and women. It was never greater.

One of the most important things young people today must

think about is that without an education, the chances of landing a good job are close to nil. The fact is that a boy or girl who quits high school before graduation has a hard time getting any but the most menial, lowest-paying jobs.

And the situation, I'm sad to report, is rapidly getting worse. You've probably heard quite a bit already about "automation." You'll hear more about that word in the future. It means using machines to do work formerly done by human beings.

Look around you now and you'll see lots of examples of automation. In offices and banks, big IBM machines have taken jobs from hundreds of thousands of bookkeepers. In the mines, machines do work for which dozens of men formerly were needed. In a prefabricated-house factory, power saws slice through dozens of pieces of lumber at once. Not long ago, to build a house, a carpenter stood with a handsaw, cutting every piece by hand. These machines do in one hour more than he could do in a week.

Everybody's looking for ways to cut out labor. Enter a new tall building and you're likely to find that the elevators are designed to run automatically. So there are fewer and fewer jobs for the men without much education who used to serve as elevator operators. In many lunchrooms, vending machines are heating and serving all kinds of prepared foods. Out the door—for good—go waiters and waitresses. Even dish washers have been replaced by automatic machines. In many places, automatic gasoline stations are being tested. Instead of having gas station attendants to fill oil tanks, you put your money in a machine and serve yourself.

Wherever you look, you'll find that ordinary jobs for people with limited education are becoming scarcer. The jobs of the future are going to go to people especially trained to handle them. For instance, in factories, men who know something about engineering will be the ones hired to take care of the machines. They will have to fix them quickly if anything goes wrong. There are plenty of jobs now—and will be in the future—for people like nurses (who need three years' experience in hospitals after high school), for teachers, for scientists, business executives, and so on. Whole new industries have grown up in recent years around the little electron tube used in radio and television but you'll need some college training, at least, to hold down the hundreds of thousands of reasonably good jobs which these industries now offer.

The point of this is that it's very desirable for a young man to get a proper education in order to provide for his family when he marries and to make proper use of the talents God has given him. To do this, he can't very well plan to marry when he's eighteen, nineteen or twenty. If he waits until his schooling is completed and he establishes himself in his career (as he should do) he won't be ready to marry until he's perhaps twenty-two or twenty-three at the earliest.

And if he's not going to marry until his mid-twenties, it makes little sense to start "going steady" when he's fourteen or fifteen. Because—and let's not forget it—"going steady" is the beginning stage of getting engaged. If you "go steady" and grow very attached to somebody, the temptation is strong to give up education, get married and settle for any sort of job— even one without any chance for advancement—just to be able to get married.

Or consider the job of being a parent today. Husbands and wives must learn a great deal more than their parents knew about the principles of child care—hygiene, vitamins, miracle drugs, etc. They are supposed to know more about how to handle a child so that he doesn't grow up a menace to society. Add it all up and this fact stares us in the face: Young men and women ought to be postponing their marriages to later years rather than rushing into them with the inadequate preparation so many have.

As a general rule, the most successful husbands and wives are those who spent their adolescent years mostly in the company of others of their own age and sex. They had a chance to develop the characteristics of their sex and learned to conduct themselves as men or women.

On the other hand, boys and girls who date too early and spend a lot of time with the other sex, sometimes do not develop the characteristics of their own sex as fully as they should. They don't have as good an understanding as they might have of what will be expected of them as men or women for the rest of their lives. In other words, their education has been neglected.

Some youngsters think they have a God-given right to date whenever they want to. This is a new idea—also a wrong one. Since time began, parents have always had the right to tell their children when they could and couldn't date. They have that right today.

If your parents think you're too young to date, they're thinking about the timetable that I described above. They may know that if you begin dating now, you may be much too young when you wind up at the altar, and much too poorly equipped to do a good job as husband and father or as a wife and mother.

5. QUALITIES IN A "DATE" THAT BOYS AND GIRLS LIKE

Ever hear of the famous recipe for rabbit stew? It begins:

"First catch a rabbit."

If you want me to give you a recipe for dating, I could begin the same way—"First find someone to date." What I mean is that you should try to make yourself attractive enough so that you'll be a welcome partner on a date.

Let's ask two questions of the girls first. What qualities do you have or can you develop that are most appealing to boys? What qualities will make boys more interested in you as a person?

There's a logical answer to this question. It goes right back to why God made two sexes. As I've pointed out, He created males and females for a purpose, and He assigned to them the characteristics they need to do better the job He wants them to do. So it's natural that boys want girls to have *feminine* qualities—those that would enable the girls to do the tasks expected of women in this world.

First of all, boys want the girls they date to be attractive physically. Again, this desire goes back to God's reasons at the time of Creation. Only when there is a physical attraction is there a desire for intimacy with the opposite sex, and only then are conditions proper for the marital act which, as you know, is necessary so that a new life can be conceived. There's nothing wrong in being interested in someone who is physically attractive—or in trying to make yourself more appealing to the other sex.

In order to be considered attractive by boys, however, a girl needn't be a raving beauty. I've heard it said by experts that any girl can use some of the hundreds of beauty aids (or is it thousands?) that are now on the market and can make herself better-looking. Even someone who hasn't been endowed with beautiful features can take care of her skin, her hair, her teeth and so on and can develop a personality that will make her whole face attractive. Some girls who haven't been given a great deal to begin with, look like the well-known "walking dream" because they make the most of what they have.

Good Looks Alone Are Not Enough

Nobody can deny that good looks are probably the most important feature that a teen-age boy looks for. But a girl with good looks and nothing else may find that she's really not very popular at all. One of the prettiest high school girls I've seen was actually the least popular member of her class. If you could hear what the boys said about her, you'd realize why. "Swollen head," "Bird brain," and "Clothes horse," were some of the milder phrases they used in describing her. As a companion on a date, these boys would gladly settle for someone less good-looking—and also less conceited.

Here's another tip, based upon the nature God gave us, about what boys like about a girl: They are drawn to one who's hard to get. The male, as the leader, wants to be the pursuer. Nothing scares him more quickly than the lass who makes it obvious that she's chasing him. As one teen-ager says, "the girl who's easy to get ain't got."

I wouldn't be so simple as to believe that an average girl doesn't move a muscle to get a date. However, she has to be subtle about it—like happening to be some place when a boy also happens to be there. You know the old saying, "A woman chases a man until he catches her." But the game is up if he suspects that he's being chased.

What's His Mother Like?

A well-known expression is that "a boy's first girl friend is his mother." He gets his first and most important impressions about women from her, and you can be sure that when he shops for a girl friend he will want her to have the qualities he has come to know in his own home. And what are those qualities?

The most feminine ones you can find: Unselfish love, sympathy, willingness to listen to his point of view, gentleness. Of course, he doesn't (or at least, shouldn't) want his girl friend to baby him as his mother might, but he wants her to show the characteristics that his mother displays. The great song favorite of years ago says it for him: "I Want a Girl Just Like the Girl Who Married Dear Old Dad."

Such a girl would be attractive, but not sexy-looking. She would have a well-scrubbed look, a pleasant smile, and makeup that was not applied with a brush.

She would be neatly dressed—neither too loud nor too soft. (You might be surprised to know what boys really think about girls who strut around in too-tight clothing, or who weigh five pounds less when they take their jewelry off, or who wear the wrong things at the wrong time.)

Girls, remember that most boys want someone who won't be conspicuous in the crowd. Yes, they want a good-looker but most of them would be annoyed with one who invited wolf whistles. They don't like to be seen with a lass who is out of place for any reason—the girl who would wear flat heels at a formal dance where high heels are called for, the girl who wears a formal evening dress when everybody else wears slacks, the girl who spends half an hour applying eye makeup just to take a trip down to the corner for a soda. One boy made a date with a girl he had never taken out before. The idea was that they would go to the movies with a group of their classmates. When he called for her, she appeared with heavy eye makeup in what seemed to be a mixture of black and blue. It was out of this world. His first question was: "Is today Halloween?"

For centuries, the philosophers of the Church have had a kind of quick, five-word guide to conduct. It is that "Virtue follows a middle course." In other words, generally the best way to handle any problem is to avoid either one extreme or the other. This is a particularly good point for girls to think about. Because despite what boys may say, they prefer a date who will not look or act in an extreme way—good or bad. Most of them have a deathly fear of being embarrassed—and they feel embarrassed by the simple process of being made the object of everybody's attention.

Qualities of Boys that Girls Like

A teacher was standing with five high school boys who were talking about how to go about getting dates. One boy after another suggested approaches that seemed to be successful with the fair sex.

"I'll give you a surefire way," the teacher said. "Just go out for the football game and score the winning touchdown in the big game of the season. Every girl in town will want to be seen with you."

The teacher was right, of course. Football heroes in high school never seem to have any trouble in persuading girls to accept their offers of dates. That also makes girls different from boys in this respect, for while most boys dislike dating a girl who is outstanding in a crowd, most girls seem to flock to the "big wheel."

To understand why this is so, we can go back once again to the different roles that God has assigned to the different sexes. In His divine plan, He made man to be the head of the house, to display qualities of leadership in order to provide for the family unit. Girls react instinctively to this condition, and naturally look toward a boy who will be a leader—a standout.

Analyze other qualities that girls like in the boys they date. You can also see how those are the very qualities that will help the male perform his God-given functions. Let me list a few:

Good looks. As in the case of what attracts boys, girls also wish to feel what has been described as the mating urge—a sense of physical desire which is necessary in every marriage.

Honesty, integrity, sincerity. A woman must be more dependent upon her husband than he is dependent upon her. By the nature of things, she must look to him for support while she remains at home caring for the family. To a great extent, her happiness depends upon how well he treats her. Consequently qualities such as these—which indicate basic strength of character—are important to her. She knows that they are the foundation of her family's life. For instance, what kind of home would there be if she never knew whether her husband would bring home his paycheck and provide the food she and her children need?

Kindness, sympathy, understanding. For long periods, an expectant mother—or one who has just given birth—may be unable to do many things for herself. She must look for gentle assistance, a cheerful word, a helping hand from her husband. She will be sad indeed if he is so wrapped up in himself, so determined to seek after his own pleasure, that he won't provide it.

The average girl may want these qualities without fully realizing why they are essential for her happiness. She usually has the good instincts that tell her that the boy who lacks these characteristics won't make a good husband. Sometimes she won't listen to her instincts and marries somebody with nothing to back up his pleasing personality.

When marriage turns sour, I've found, the husband, or wife can look back to dating days and see that they had plenty of warning signs. But they closed their eyes to the undesirable signs they saw.

Look for the Human Qualities

There are other qualities that girls seek in boys—and boys seek in girls—which are not directly related to their sex. These are the human qualities. After all, while boys and girls bear the different characteristics of their sex, they also share common qualities as creatures of God. These qualities include such things as:

A sense of humor—the ability to see the wry side of life and to find something to laugh about even when the going gets rough.

A sense of justice—a desire to see that nobody is exploited or "pushed around" and that everybody is entitled to his fair due.

A desire to please—the willingness to do things to make other people happy, to give as well as take and thus to get along with people.

And above all, *respect for one's self and respect for others*—a realization that every human being has certain rights under God. The boy or girl who can inspire true love is the one who will help (or at least, not hinder) another person's pursuit of happiness on earth and in heaven.

As a concluding thought on this subject, let me say that I don't agree with some authorities who like to apply a slide rule to a boy, or girl, to decide whether he would make a suitable dating, marriage partner. Science is wonderful, and very often it can show young people in a general way exactly what their chances are for marital success if they pursue a certain course of action.

But in every good marriage—and therefore, in every successful dating combination—there is a mysterious power of attraction. This strange, mysterious magnetism may draw a boy and girl together in a way that defies all the analyses of the scientists. If the modern workers in a laboratory tried to pin a label on this ingredient, they might come up with something like the name of the stuff they put in toothpaste—something like DL72. Common folks, however, might say that this mysterious attraction is "a meeting of hearts," and let it go at that.

Unselfishness: Key to Friendship

On one Sunday in January every year, a special ceremony is held in the great Cathedral of St. Patrick in New York. With Francis Cardinal Spellman presiding, there usually are hundreds of couples in the cathedral all with one thing in common: They have been married for exactly half a century. In the ceremony, His Eminence awards scrolls of recognition to the couples who have survived the hazards of married life for such a long period and who can hold hands knowing that each has contributed to the holiness and happiness of the other.

I've talked to many of the couples who have been married all these years, and I've been able to detect certain qualities that they seem to have in common—qualities necessary, I think, for any two people to live together in harmony.

There's no question in my mind that one characteristic stands out not only in men and women observing a golden wedding anniversary, but in practically every other couple who give signs of being happily married. That quality is unselfishness—the willingness to make sacrifices for others.

Large doses of unselfishness are necessary for boys and girls on a date as well as for men and women in a marriage. Let's say, for the sake of an example, that one hundred pounds are needed. I suppose a friendship could survive if one person contributed the entire hundred pounds and the other contributed nothing. Or if the person made most of the sacrifices and contributed 80 percent of the unselfishness while the other gave only 20 percent. But the happiest relationship for both parties is when both contribute an equal share. When that happens, it means that both the boy and girl are aware of the other's needs and desires and have the goodness of heart to try to satisfy them.

You'll have a long way to go before you celebrate your golden wedding anniversary. (Maybe when that time comes, your grandchildren will finance a little trip to enable you to spend a weekend or so in that new luxury hotel on the moon.) But one thing is certain. It is that the spirit of unselfishness will be just as important to your future as it has been to all the couples who come to the altar at St. Patrick's to be greeted by their Archbishop.

You Needn't Be a "Door Mat"

Is being unselfish the same as "letting people play you for a sucker"? Of course not. You have certain rights and privileges that you should not hand over just because someone wants you to. Let's say you've worked to earn enough money to buy an ice cream soda. Someone else sits back and mopes while you work. Then he asks you to turn over all the money so that he can have the soda. You'd be a fool to do so. Or suppose a girl allows a boy to take liberties with her person just because he asks to. She wouldn't be unselfish—just downright stupid.

But there is a spirit of generosity that we all can cultivate toward other people. It's really a strong sense of charity—a desire to help others achieve good. Let's have some examples:

Your friend has had an accident. Now he's in the hospital, all bandaged, with no one to talk to. You know you won't enjoy the sight of him because he looks like something out of a horror film, but you're willing to forget your own feelings to help make him a little happier.

Your date is set on seeing a movie that won't play in your town again for months, if ever. But you've already seen the movie. An unselfish person might shrug and decide to see the film again. He is willing to compromise.

Someone who must always have his own way, quickly gets shunned by anyone who can do so. Here again, the instinct of a boy or girl to keep away from a selfish individual is a sound one. Because the "me first" party who marries will want his own way in everything—and will be a terrible scourge to have to live with day after day.

Unselfishness—or its opposite—often shows up in conversation. Count the number of I's a boy or girl uses in a five-minute conversation, and you may have a fairly good idea of what he thinks of himself. Some people are so wrapped up in their little world that they couldn't recognize anything else if it were announced with fire sirens. All they can think about are their own interests and desires—and their conversation proves it.

In class one time, a boy was supposed to type a term paper. He told his teacher he couldn't do it because his typewriter wouldn't work—the key that printed the letter "I" was broken. The class howled at his unconscious humor. But if a law were passed tomorrow preventing the use of the letter I, a lot of people would discover that they couldn't speak the language.

When a person is always preoccupied with himself, he can't spend the time to consider the legitimate wants of others. So he's insensitive—unable to give the sympathy and understanding that one friend should always expect of another, and that a married person should be able to expect of a mate.

Eleven Words to Guide You

Is there any little principle to tell you when you should be unselfish and self-sacrificing, and when it might be a mistake to do so? Some guide to tell you when it is right and honorable to make compromises, and when you woud be a chump to do so?

There is such a guide. It has been tested and proved for centuries. Our Lord taught it, and it has just eleven words: "Do unto others as you would have them do unto you." Observe this Golden Rule, and you will have a key that unlocks the door to friendship with the opposite sex and also with members of your own.

6. THE PEOPLE YOU SHOULDN'T DATE

A priest was conducting a pre-Cana conference—a course for men and women about to be married. He asked the couples present to tell how they first met, and how long they had dated before they became engaged.

They had met under a wide variety of circumstances. Some first saw each other at school, at school dances or other school events. Some had been introduced by mutual friends. Some met at a place of business where both worked. Some knew each other from childhood. They had dated from four months to several years before they decided to hook up for life.

The priest then asked if anyone in the hall had wanted to marry the partner-to-be from the very first time they dated. Not a hand was raised. If he had asked a thousand couples the same question, I doubt whether results would have been different.

As I mentioned earlier, the usual pattern is for a couple to date a few times. On these dates they learn what they can about each other's basic interests, personality, etc. Only after a large number of dates could anyone really decide whether the other person was worth the risk of a lifetime.

The point of all this is that when you go out on a date, there's some possibility that the person you go with will ultimately be standing with you at the marriage rail. So it follows that you shouldn't date anyone you are sure you wouldn't want to be married to. Why not? Because one date leads to another. Before you know it, you're "in love" and "going steady." And from "going steady" there's only a short step to engagement and marriage.

One trouble with this process is that when you're in love you're liable to forget a great deal that you ought to remember.

You're likely to overlook a great many hazards that might give your marriage little chance of succeeding.

Such a hazard exists when the party of the second part practices a different religion. I don't care what religion is involved. Any mixed marriage has less chance of succeeding than one in which both persons hold the same beliefs about the most important facts of life—why we were born, Who made us, what happens to us after death. A Catholic who marries a Protestant, a Jew, a member of any other religion—or someone with no religion at all—is bound to encounter different beliefs about how life should be lived. Those beliefs will result in differences of opinion about how your children should be educated and in hundreds of other ways.

"Experience Is the Best Teacher"

Why does the Church warn against mixed marriages—marrying somebody who does not practice the same religion as yourself? She does it because she knows from experience that such a marriage makes it more difficult to gain the most important goal of life—the salvation of your soul. She knows that the Catholic frequently loses the Faith entirely, or waters it down by forgetting about the sacraments, missing Mass and tossing over the rules of God and the Church.

The non-Catholic partner often waters down his or her own religion as well. The result: An unhappy "no man's land" where neither practices the religion he or she was taught, and both run the risk of damnation.

Where there's a mixed marriage, the danger to the faith of a child is even greater. One careful survey found that it often happens that the child born in a mixed marriage is never baptized or grows up learning little or nothing about his religion. He's less likely to go to a Catholic school. When he himself marries, he's more likely to marry outside the Faith.

Even if you don't care about losing your own soul, would you like to see your child lose his?

It's true that there are mixed marriages in which the Catholic partner continues to be a good—even a great—Catholic, and in which the children grow up to be a marvelous credit to our religion. These cases happen much less often, though, than the other kind I've mentioned. The law of averages is against them.

Of course, the Church primarily wants you to save your soul when she warns you about the moral danger of mixed marriages. But she's also interested in your happiness on earth. Mixed marriages tell a sad story there, too.

Tales that Cold Figures Tell

Statistics (what would we do without them?) show that rates of both divorce and separation are three times greater when Catholics marry non-Catholics than when both parties are members of the same Faith. Even when a husband and wife remain together, their different attitudes about religion often cause trouble that may not be serious enough to break up the marriage but makes the going rough at times. As a Protestant minister once commented: "Marriage is tough for people of the same religion. Why complicate it more than you have to?"

For example, there is a Protestant woman who is married to a fine Jewish man, who is as decent a person as you'd want to meet. He is a devoted husband and a kind father. He wouldn't willingly hurt anybody in his life. If you looked at that family as an outsider, you might think that everybody was perfectly happy.

What you don't know is that the man's parents are always making comments about her religion, and that her parents and friends always make comments about his. They were both unhappy about where they were married. She had to give up her personal belief, marrying before a justice of the peace because he refused to be married in a church. And his mother and father were caused great sorrow because she refused to be married before a rabbi. 1209379

She can't bring up her children as Christian and he can't bring them up as Jews. The youngsters don't know how to celebrate Christmas, because their father doesn't believe in it. And they don't celebrate the sacred holy days of his religion, because their mother does not believe in them.

So both the man and woman go through life, both unable to realize the things that are sacred to them. Believe me, they're both mighty unhappy about it. For example, the woman said that if she had her life to live over again, despite the fact that her husband was a wonderful man, she could not pay the price of giving up the things that she held sacred in her religion to marry him. I'm sure he feels the same way.

Right now, you'd probably agree with priests, ministers and rabbis, all of whom turn thumbs down on mixed marriage. So how can you make sure you won't get involved in one? The best way is to adopt one simple rule: Don't date non-Catholics. This three-word rule is absolutely foolproof. As we saw from the experience of the engaged couples, if you don't date, you won't mate.

Let me make it very plain that in opposing mixed marriages, I have nothing against non-Catholic boys or girls as individuals. Probably all of us know Protestants and Jews who are more respectable, and better representatives of their religions, than many so-called Catholics. My point is *not* that a Catholic is better than anybody else, but that he's different. He has a different idea about the most basic questions in life—questions that will grow larger, instead of smaller, the older he becomes. No matter how good and decent a non-Catholic may be, this difference can wreck a marriage as well as the people in it.

The "Fast Crowd"

No matter how things change, one class of persons—generally middle-aged—will always be with us. When I was young, these persons were described as "hrrmphers." Their specialty was to look at what young people were doing and remark: "Hrrmph! What's the younger generation coming to?"

In earlier days, the carburetor Charlies who drove their Stanley steamers down the road at eight miles an hour undoubtedly excited such comment. In the Twenties, "flappers" who did the Charleston provoked similar remarks, although many of the "flappers" have turned into the staid parents of today. Maybe some of them now even wonder where today's young folks are heading. Teen-agers who wore bobby socks and spent hours outside theaters awaiting their chance to swoon at Frank Sinatra are dignified mothers and fathers of the kindergarten set of today. So it goes. You youngsters who get the Hrrmph treatment today may well be the "hrrmphers" of tomorrow.

What the headshakers usually fail to keep in mind is that a big distinction can be made between what's a matter of taste and what's a matter of morals. After all, listening to rock 'n' roll records because you like the rhythm (what rhythm?) really has nothing to do with your moral life. You could listen all you wanted and still approach the altar rail on Sunday. On the other hand, it's possible to be devoted to Brahms and Beethoven and still live in sin. It's that way with most of the fads of the day. I'm less concerned about how the current crop of high school students wear their hair, about who their current movie or TV favorites are, than I am in whether they're leading good, holy lives.

There's a big difference—a difference I'm sure you're aware of. Because someone doesn't like your certain type of music or particular type of headdress doesn't necessarily mean that you're on the road to damnation.

When I talk about a "fast crowd," I don't think of those who get off to a quick start at a traffic light. Nor do I refer to those who dance twice as fast as other people. One group of youngsters enjoyed taking dance records, running them at the fastest possible speed on their three-way victrolas, and trying to keep up with the tempo. That's one trick old-timers had better try at their own risk.

When I speak of a "fast crowd," I mean those who play fast and loose with the moral code—those who go further than they should with the opposite sex, those who are often teetering on the brink of immorality.

Young people have a very sharp sense about this, I've found. You know exactly what conduct is chaste and proper. Perhaps better than an adult, a youngster often knows in his heart what kind of dress is modern but "safe"—and what kind is calculated to excite wrong ideas in the opposite sex.

"Birds of a Feather Flock Together"

If I wanted to find out something about any group of youngsters, I'm sure their friends and acquaintances would have a pretty good idea of what they're doing—whether members of the group generally act within the framework of the moral law or whether the members seek pleasures that are either wrong themselves or could easily lead to sin.

You yourself probably know it if any crowd drinks too much, necks too much, thinks too little about the ideals of Christian life, looks too eagerly for forbidden thrills. Whether this crowd runs around in convertibles or jalopies, wears hair long or short, listens to folk songs or jazz—regardless of these incidentals, if it's violating the moral law or is in danger of doing so, it's the one for you to steer clear of.

Not that you should associate with people with tastes en-

tirely different from your own. You don't have to pal with
boys and girls who won't read anything but a comic book just
because he or she is a good Christian. But you might try to
form friendships with good Christians who have your own
tastes in other matters too.

In the last showdown, the gang you go with will be the
crowd that thinks about marriage as you do. Or, rather you'll
think the same as the gang does. Young people who think
marriage was designed by God for a sacred purpose, obviously won't think that chastity is an old-fashioned notion.
Instead, they'll fully realize why it is of basic importance.
Their actions will follow their ideals and they'll lead Christian
lives in preparing for marriage.

If you're in that group, you'll do the same. Because if
there's one characteristic young people have in abundance,
it's a desire to be like those they associate with. You'll want
to wear pretty much the same kind of clothes, the same type of
haircut, eat the same kinds of foods, see the same movies as
your friends. There's nothing wrong with that. I mention it
only to urge you to use your "desire to conform" to good advantage. When you do, you'll find that doing things the Christian way comes to you much more easily.

A favorite story of mine that illustrates this point perfectly,
concerns traveling conditions in the pioneer days out West.
The first wagons that crossed the prairie naturally had to
make their own roads. Then other wagons came along and
found themselves in the grooves made by their predecessors.
Finally the grooves turned into deep ruts. Things reached such
a point that stagecoach companies warned their drivers:
"Choose your ruts carefully. You'll be in them for twenty-
five miles."

Choosing your companions is like that. You'll be in their
groove, following the path they follow. If their way leads to
your sanctity, fine. But if you choose a group that travels
along the path of easy morality, you'll find your road strewn
with heartbreak and disaster.

7. SOME DO'S FOR DATERS

One high school counselor who knows teen-agers very well, says that the great enemy of a good time on a date is boredom. If boys and girls have nothing constructive to do or nothing interesting to talk about, they'll soon be sitting around twiddling their thumbs, hoping the party breaks up early or entertaining wild ideas about how to whip up some excitement. Some of the ideas may be good ones, but some may be offbeat or even off limits.

Before you make a date, devote a little thought to all the good things you could do. You'll uncover a world of possibilities:

Take part in sports in season. Except in the most miserable weather, there's usually something you can do outdoors: Swimming in summer, tennis most months of the year, skiing or ice-skating in winter. Many communities also have roller-skating rinks that are open most of the year.

Watch sporting events. In most fair-sized towns, there are usually at least a few events on weekends—your own school team, perhaps, or class teams are playing. If you live in a large community, there may be professional sport events to attend. Cheap seats at these usually aren't beyond a teen-ager's reach.

Help somebody. In one village one of the juniors in high school was left fatherless. His mother had a hard time caring for her five children, and when it came time to paint the house, the junior's friends of both sexes arrived with rollers and brushes. After a day's work was done, there was a cookout in the yard. "I never felt so good about helping somebody, or had such a good time doing it," one lad commented. There's always somebody who needs a helping hand. When one person helps alone, it may be drudgery. When a group does it, it's fun.

Cook a community meal. One youngster can bring the hot dogs, another the rolls, a third the potato chips. Or the girls might get together and cook for the boys. Maybe some lads who fancy themselves skilled with a skillet may be persuaded to whip up a spaghetti dinner for their girl friends.

One thing can be said for dates that involve preparing meals. Everybody gets to know who the good cooks are. If the way to a man's heart is through his stomach, as has often been said, the girl who's a whiz in the kitchen may discover that her skill will make her more attractive to the opposite gender.

Learn something in a group. Again, what might be dull for one can be great fun for a few. You might try to master dancing, for example—or at least learn to do the new steps that are always coming out. I've known of groups who've had wonderful times learning card games (proficiency at bridge seems to be a must at many colleges) and also improving themselves in golf, tennis and the like. If your school doesn't have special-interest clubs, maybe you can start one. For instance, get together the boys and girls interested in photography, science, art, or other subjects.

Listen to records. All that's needed is a phonograph. Let all members of the group contribute their favorite disks. Add a few bottles of soda, peanuts and popcorn, and you can have a high time at low cost.

Hold a plain, old-fashioned gabfest. Many teen-agers get as much pleasure out of bull sessions as anything else. Just sitting around and swapping ideas and ambitions is, in fact, a favorite pastime of college students. It's possible that you'll learn a great deal at such sessions. You'll also learn to appreciate logical thinking and to distinguish the shallow thinker from the one who can back his ideas with solid reasoning. The real character of an individual—what he's like, what he truly believes, what he hopes to get from life—often is revealed more vividly in a two-hour bull session than in hours of other activities.

Three Ways to Have More Fun on a Date

The above are but a few of the things you can do that are enjoyable, inexpensive, and constructive. If you want to add more to your dating pleasure, follow these three suggestions:

1. Always date in groups. You'll find it much more fun to do things together. If one person feels "a little down," there are others to cheer him up. When more persons are doing things together, there's much less chance of boredom.

2. Plan activities in advance. Sometimes a little preparation can make the difference between an enjoyable time and a washout. A group of sophomores thought it might be fun to go roller-skating. One phone call would have established that the rink was closed that night. After they learned the bad news at the rink, they had nothing more to do than sit around all night twisting soda straws. Had they planned more carefully, they might have uncovered the fact that a rousing basketball game was being played not far away, where they would have found more fun.

If you plan events carefully, you'll be aware of what time the event begins and when it ends—an important point to use in getting your parents' permission when that's necessary. You'll also be able to tie in with the transportation schedules. You won't have to walk home at night because you've missed the last bus by five minutes.

3. Let your parents know your plans. A boy should always call for the girl at her home and let her parents meet him. He should ask what time they wish her back and should escort her home at the stated time. If an unforeseen delay occurs (no buses are running, the car has a flat tire, etc.) he should phone them so they won't worry.

Let's look a little more closely at that Rule Number One.

There's Safety in Numbers

Boys and girls of my own generation—around the time of Thomas Jefferson, it seems—had an easier way of avoiding temptation than do youngsters of the present day. The reason? They had a different way of dating. They generally went out in groups.

On a Saturday night, perhaps, three boys and three girls would go together to the local skating rink, the local amusement park or local movie. No particular boy went out with a particular girl, and no lass was considered anyone's "girl friend." Everybody went out together, and everybody had a good time.

There was no pairing off—no feeling that any person "belonged" to anyone of the opposite sex. There was no tendency to plan individual dates, no tendency to "go steady." And there was no tendency to go overboard on necking.

That is the real danger when a boy and girl go out on a date alone. They are more likely to become bored with ordinary pleasures than if they are in a group, and more likely to begin investigating the extremes of kissing, or worse. They find themselves beset by temptations they would not encounter if they were in the company of other youngsters. For this reason, you should try to avoid solitary dates and should realize that there is usually "Safety in Numbers."

When you participate in group dating, you may be interested to know, you will be doing something for your own protection that has been found necessary down through the ages. Every culture, from ancient times to the recent past, has deemed it important to set up safeguards to keep temptations away from young people.

In some parts of Asia, for example, they still take an extreme position, and simply refuse to let boys and girls associate with each other. As you know, parents there often serve as matchmakers, and a bridegroom and bride-to-be sometimes don't meet each other until their wedding day. In some Latin countries, there is still the institution of the chaperon. Respectable young people cannot date unless they are accompanied by an older person whom the girl's parents trust.

In some parts of our own country, boys are not permitted to date a girl unless her parents first give him a thorough, exhaustive examination. They may even make a close scrutiny of his pedigree for a few generations back.

Generally speaking, however, these safeguards have all been discarded. I don't think anyone is shedding too many tears over this fact. But the reason the safeguards were found necessary in the first place—to protect young people from temptations that arise when they date alone—is still with us. Dating in pairs or in groups, it seems to me, is one way that youngsters themselves can maintain the protection they need without having their parents or older persons around to make sure that they toe the line.

You can recognize why there is safety in numbers if you first consider the basic reason why couples pair off. The only real reason for it is the attraction that a boy feels for a particular girl, and vice versa. But don't fool yourself. At the root of this attraction is the natural attraction of sex that one feels for the other.

It is sometimes a revealing thing to observe married couples when, for example, they get together at someone's home for an evening. You usually will find that the men carry on a conversation on one side of the room, while the women converge on the other. That seems to prove rather clearly that when the question of the physical attraction of women does not arise, men would much rather associate with other men. When a man does associate with a woman alone, what draws them together is the fact that they have different sexes. In fact, when boys and girls commit sins of impurity, it will be found that they have first strayed from the crowd.

Girls particularly should keep the dangers of "pairing off" clearly in mind. They can control the circumstances under which they agree to go out with boys. If a girl is asked for a date, she can skillfully arrange to make it a double date and can plan matters so that the temptation to sneak off alone will not arise. The boy who turns down the idea of a double date can be suspected of having dishonorable intentions in mind.

Some girls will consider the advice in the above paragraph as old hat. They will argue that they can control a boy without any outside help, and that they can stop him from "going too far" whenever they want. This statement is the one usually held by girls before they lose their virtue. It comes under the heading of "Famous Last Words."

It is not generally known that while a female's desires are aroused more slowly than a male's, she can quickly lose control of herself once she allows these desires to gain momentum. She may soon find herself completely engulfed by them, with no capacity to stop.

A famous woman doctor says that this myth—that a woman can stop whenever she wants to—is responsible for numerous pregnancies among unmarried girls. Dr. Marion Hilliard, chief of obstetrics and gynecology at the Women's College Hospital of Toronto, states flatly that a woman's first and best defense against such a tragedy is to have no confidence at all in her ability to turn lovemaking on and off like a faucet.

One of the greatest ways to avoid trouble of any kind is to listen to the advice of people older and wiser than yourself. Dr. Hilliard knows what she is talking about, because in her work she has encountered hundreds of cases of unmarried expectant mothers. I suggest that you take her word in this case. The price of experience, of learning these facts the hard way, is far greater than any sane person would want to pay.

Boys might heed the words that came from the lips of a little Italian woman with six sons. Whenever one left the house on a date, she made it a ritual to pat him on the head, kiss him and say: "Remember, your girl has a mother who worries about her too."

Her thought is one every boy might remember. When he takes out a girl, he has a responsibility for her welfare. He should try to provide an agreeable time that both will remember without regrets.

Temptations and Sin

When you received the sacrament of Confirmation, you were made a soldier of Christ. You joined with Him in the battle against sin.

You probably regarded the enemy as someone outside yourself. It is true that such enemies of Christianity are all around us—those who would destroy our faith in God, who urge us to disregard His laws, who try to tell us that the Ten Commandments mean nothing and that we should all do what we want when we want to do it.

The greatest enemy you will encounter in your struggle to save your soul, however, is your own nature. If you want to serve victoriously in the Army of Christ, you must first build up your resistance so that you can turn aside all the temptations to commit sin that will confront you.

Make no mistake about it: Not only as a teen-ager, but throughout your lifetime, you will have many temptations to overcome. In fact, probably no day will ever pass without at least a minor temptation—perhaps a whisper from Satan urging you to tell a lie, cheat a little, disobey your lawful superiors a little, or to commit at least a venial sin. You may often be tempted by impure thoughts and desires and by urges to violate the Sixth Commandment by yourself or with another person.

You need not be ashamed of these temptations. They come to all of us. Our Lord Himself was tempted with the world if He would bow down and worship Satan. Of course, Jesus rebuffed the devil. And it is right here—in whether or not we resist temptation—that the story of our own success or failure in life will be written.

In dating, the greatest temptation will be to commit sins of impurity. These temptations may arise from something you have done deliberately—excessive kissing, for example. But they can also arise without any voluntary action on your part. A boy may suddenly become beset by impure desires as a result of sniffing a perfume. (Judging from their ads, some are made for that specific purpose.) Or a touch or a glance from a girl may do it. A girl may suddenly find herself with desires as a result of viewing a romantic scene in a movie, or simply by watching the moonlight.

Some American Indians had this expression: "Fool me once, shame on you; fool me twice, shame on me." They meant, that the first time the unexpected happened, they perhaps couldn't be held fully to blame because they had no previous experience to warn them. If the same thing happened a second time, they could not use this excuse, however. They should have learned their lesson from before.

You might apply the Indians' yardstick in dealing with temptations. The first time you are tempted as a result of contact with a certain person, place or thing, you might claim that you didn't know better. The second time, you no longer have that excuse. So shame on you.

In discussing this subject with youngsters, I have discovered that it is not necessary to dot every "i" at great length. Better than anyone else, you know what circumstances tend to induce impure thoughts in your mind. It may be a certain girl, a certain type of book or movie, a certain place, certain companions of your own sex—you know where the trouble areas lie. And better than anyone else, you know what persons, places and things you must avoid if temptations—and possible future sins—also are to be avoided.

The best way to handle these involuntary temptations is to

try to change the subject immediately. If you can, indulge in some physical activity. Find someone to talk to. Phone a friend. Repair something of yours that needs fixing.

Have you ever been tempted to sin in the midst of an exciting basketball game? While running a race? While watching a thrilling adventure series on television? It is unlikely, because your mind is occupied and there is no room for temptations to enter.

A teacher used to tell his class, "People with one head can think of only one thing at a time." So if you have only one head, you'll resist temptation if you put your mind to work on other subjects. Remember the comparison with the water pipes I mentioned earlier? Your mind is like the faucet that turns the water in your kitchen on and off. You can develop it so that you can turn away from any evil thoughts that may come to your mind.

Never treat temptations lightly. They are like the baby gorilla a man made a pet of. Day by day, the man watched it turn from a playful animal into a brawny creature. Daily it grew stronger and more threatening. One day the man went to pet it and it clawed him to death. So it is with temptation. If you harbor it and take pleasure from it, you will soon discover that it has overpowered you.

8. THE IMPORTANCE OF CHASTITY

One of the great privileges of life is your ability to share with God the continuing work of creation. Of the many precious gifts He has given you, the faculties of reproduction are assuredly pearls of great price, and the sexual passions involved in their use deserve your utmost respect and concern.

Suppose you were given a precious diamond. You wouldn't toss it into a bureau drawer reserved for broken pencils and paper; you'd put it in a strong box and make sure no one had access to it. If you were growing a precious flower, you wouldn't transplant it onto a garbage pile. If you received the highest medal of honor your country could bestow, you wouldn't leave it where children could play with it. Yet the gift of reproduction is greater by far than any of these things.

Like all great powers, sexual passion can be used for good or evil. It's used for good when it's used in the way God intended when He gave it to you. It's used for evil when it's used in defiance of His will.

Once again, we must ask a basic question: What use does God want you to make of your reproductive faculties? Because it is such a powerful thing, it obviously must be used only under certain specific circumstances. Since He intended it as a means of creating new human lives, it's obvious that it may be used only by those who are prepared to care for a child and to spend years educating him until he can care for himself. Only married persons, and they alone, meet that requirement.

You will need to guard your integrity until the time when these powers can be properly used. There is nothing unusual about that. Consider the greatest gift of man—the ability to participate in the miraculous change of bread and wine into the Body and Blood of Our Lord. This gift is so great that only those who are ordained can touch the Sacred Host. The young seminarian may not do so until that great moment when he receives the sacrament of Holy Orders. Your body, too, is a sacred object—one that should be touched only by those who, through the sacrament of Matrimony, have received the right from God to do so.

I could cite dozens of cases, which we all accept, in which unauthorized persons must keep "hands off." For instance, we all know of drugs, when taken under strict supervision, that can save lives. Used improperly, they can cause death. So, to safeguard their use, society says they can be prescribed only by a trained, qualified doctor.

Consider how the use of an automobile is safeguarded. A car is a great means of taking you where you want to go in a hurry. But it's also a murder weapon if put in the hands of someone who can't drive properly. That's why drivers must be licensed. Take another example—the use of dynamite. No one in his right mind would suggest that it be sold in toy shops for kiddies to play with. Yet it's a great boon to mankind when used properly. We'd have a tough time building highways without it.

Chastity Is for All Ages

To safeguard the dynamite which is his sexual nature, we say that a person must exercise chastity. Now, "chastity" is a word that many Americans don't like. The way some of them react when they hear it, you would almost think it was a dirty word. Enemies of God, religion and, I might add, human decency, say that it means "no fun." In their minds, chastity means a pleasureless existence. Or when good people hear the word, they immediately think of priests and nuns.

Sometimes the best of us believe that the wedding ceremony is merely the permission given married people to be "unchaste," for chastity seems to be equated with sexlessness.

Let us get certain facts straight.

Chastity is a human virtue. Like any virtue, it enables us to do something rightly. (And it is important that civilized human beings, not to say Christian, do things rightly—i.e., have virtue.) For example, the virtue of temperance or moderation empowers us to eat and drink what we need to live, tells us not to consume harmful foods and liquids, inhibits us from eating too much or too little. The drunkard, like the murderer, the adulterer, or the lustful man, is intemperate—and the intemperate man is to that extent a bad man. Like the bad apple, he does not measure up to what he ought to be.

When it comes to regulating our sexual appetites, virtue is also necessary. In this case the virtue is called chastity.

Let us take a look at what the world would be like without chastity. People could indulge their lowest natures in any way, at any time, with anybody. Pretty horrible thought, isn't it? Without chastity, we'd be somewhat worse than animals. After all, God has imposed certain restraints even on the dumb animal. Only certain animals can mate with each other. There are times when animals cannot mate at all.

But man! God has turned human sexuality completely over to our Adams and Eves. And because man is made to God's image and likeness, is spiritual and is free, all that God has said to us is this:

"You know how I want these powers to be used. Now use them intelligently (I gave you a mind) and use them morally (I am your Father)."

What then is chastity?

It is the virtue whereby we use our sexual powers intelligently and reasonably, as God wishes them to be used, certainly not against His Will, in moderation, and according to our state in life.

Let us consider first "our state in life." Married people are authorized to use these faculties, because marriage was invented by God for the procreation and education of children and the temporal happiness of the couple who commit themselves to this sacred work. The use of sex in marriage, therefore, is itself sacred.

Does this mean that for the married, "anything goes"? Not at all. A married man or woman may well be a sex glutton or may engage in unnatural acts. They may be offensive in their lovemaking. Or practice contraception. Or become adulterers. If they do any of these things—if they do not use intelligence, reason and moderation in the exercise of their marital rights—they are wrong.

Must married people be chaste? Of course. And chastity for the married sometimes may mean that the faculties of sex *not be used*. For example, when the wife is sick, or is about to have a baby, or the husband is away from home on business. We would not think much of married people who acted otherwise.

Now for people who are unmarried, chastity (again the reasonable use of sex according to God's Will) means that the sexual faculties may not be used at all. This applies to religious, the widowed, and all single men and women.

Chastity, then, makes us masters of our passions—not their slaves. Chastity makes us truly human because it accentuates the spirit of man, not his body. Unchastity, on the other hand, whether in the married or the single, says that we live by the urges of our body unreasonably, and lack the control or moderation we expect of anyone who would represent the best in God's humanity.

This does not mean that a chaste man or woman lacks sexual drives. How silly can you get? The world and the devil, as well as the flesh itself, will test your fiber. You will be tempted constantly to use these faculties stupidly and immorally. And in this contest, you should be prepared to use your most resolute and determined efforts—just as you'd use your most determined efforts to guard a precious diamond.

Probably the most important thing you should know to maintain your chastity is that you have the power to do it.

When God gave you a will, He gave you the tool you need to resist temptation and to live free of sin.

Many young people don't understand this simple fact and therefore they find themselves unable to resist the temptations that they allow to come their way. They seem to think that because sexual temptations are physical and affect the body, for example, that there's little or nothing the mind can do about them. But always remember this all-important point: You'll never succumb to temptations unless your mind gives consent. You'll never be guilty of sin unless your mind gives you the go-ahead signal.

In your house, you probably have a supply of water coming in from outside—from a spring, maybe, or from a public reservoir. That water is in the pipes at all times. But you don't have to let it run into your sink if you don't want to. You can turn it off just by turning off the faucet that controls its flow.

The physical power to engage in the act of sex, which God has given you, can be compared to that pipewater, at least in this one respect. It will be used or not used as your will dictates.

Why is it so important to remember that your mind is where your fight for chastity will be won? Because if you know exactly how temptations can be thwarted, you can use all your energy where it will do the most good. *Control your mind and everything else will take care of itself.*

Want a little demonstration of how mastery over a control point can mean the difference between victory and defeat? Just step into a ring sometime with a master of the art of Judo. Whether the expert is a man or woman, tall or short, muscular or flabby, he or she could throw you on your back in a few seconds—just by hitting you where you're most vulnerable. "A chain is only as strong as its weakest link," remember. Suppose you were attacked by a giant, six feet, four inches tall and weighing three hundred pounds—a mass of man in the pink of condition. Could you defend yourself? Yes—if you knew Judo. Even little old ladies have done it.

You might concentrate all your energy in one place, for example, and grab him by his little finger. You could cause him excruciating pain and have him on his knees, begging for mercy, because by gaining mastery over one small part of the body, you gained mastery over its entirety. (Warning: You could easily break his finger this way, so it's not something to do just for the fun of it.)

Now let's see how control of your mind means control of your sex impulses. When you were only a few years old, you could have seen pictures of the opposite sex that to an adult would be downright pornographic. But to you, they were meaningless. Why? Because *your mind* gave them absolutely no significance.

Or suppose that today you were to look at people who in other parts of the world might be regarded as very tempting. Look at a woman or man from Asia or Africa, for example, who might be the glamorous ones of their continent. Chances are that you would not find them appealing in the least, any more than an Asian or African would be able to figure out what we see in some of our movie stars. A person with great sex appeal in Africa would seem to lack same in Alaska, and vice versa.

So what makes a man or woman attractive from a physical point of view? It's the mind of the beholder—and nothing else.

Take another example. Suppose there is a nightclub with striptease performers. A boy brought up in one environment might find the performance so revolting that nothing would be less likely to arouse his sexual desires. On the other hand, a boy looking for sexual excitement might find it there—because his mind wanted to.

Develop Good Lifetime Habits

Practices you develop in maintaining your chastity can serve you all your life. Learn how to control your thoughts—to recognize when they're straying into dangerous territory, and to change them abruptly as soon as you realize what they are. (One of the best ways, as I have mentioned, is to indulge in physical exercises. You can "change the subject" by making a phone call and talking to somebody else, or by striking up a conversation on a different subject. Try to think of other things to rid your mind of impure thoughts.)

Also try to recognize, in advance, situations that will cause unchaste thoughts to enter your mind. Perhaps you'll notice that association with certain persons creates these thoughts, or that the tempting thoughts come when you attend certain movies or read certain books or magazines. Stay away from persons, places or things where you know you'll have such temptations.

A girl who'd had several dates with a boy knew he was heading in one direction—one in which she didn't want to go. It would have been foolish and dangerous to try to argue with him when he got started necking, so she took the safest way out: The next time he called for a date, she turned him down. A teen-age lad had discovered some smutty magazines on the rack of his local drugstore, and he found himself wondering what was inside those obscene covers. He knew that the magazines had been published with the sole objective of exciting passion, and he knew that he'd have to protect himself by staying away from that drugstore in the future.

In realizing that controlling your mind is the only way to control your body, always keep this thought in front of you: You can achieve chastity if you want to and if you try to. A good story about this is one told concerning Admiral Samuel F. Du Pont in the Civil War. You may remember that Du Pont had been instructed to lead his ships into the Charleston harbor but failed to do so. Later he was called before Admiral David Glasgow ("Damn the Torpedoes") Farragut to tell what had happened.

Du Pont had all sorts of excuses. The harbor defenses were too powerful, his ships were not sufficiently protected, and so on and so on.

After listening to all of these excuses, Admiral Farragut remarked: "There's another reason. *You didn't believe you could do it.*"

It's a well-known principle of psychology that if you want to succeed at anything, you have to believe you can do it. Say you wanted to learn how to drive a car. What chance would you have if you kept telling yourself you couldn't do it?

Of course, you wouldn't start out with the idea that it would be impossible, or even difficult. True, you don't expect to get behind the wheel, shift noiselessly, and take off smoothly. You'll have some hard moments—just as you had hard moments learning to ride a bicycle or to roller-skate. But what will carry you through and make you a capable driver is your confidence that you'll learn with practice. And also your determination—because you know that having an operator's license in your hands will make the task of learning worth while.

So with chastity. As I mentioned above, chastity is something you'll need all your life. Even when you're married, you won't be able to engage in the act of sex whenever you want to. For example, when a wife is expecting a baby, marital relations are often severely restricted during the early months of her pregnancy and almost always are prohibited during the last six weeks of it as well as for a few weeks after the baby is born. And, if married people have legitimate reasons for limiting the size of their family, they must abstain from relations on the several days each month when the conception of a child could occur.

Your knowledge of how to maintain your chastity is a little like learning to operate a car. Once you master the technique and continue to practice it, you'll find that it becomes easier and easier.

Only rarely does a person lose chastity without warning. What usually happens is that the individual involved has entertained impure thoughts and has dwelt upon them in great detail. An act of sin almost always begins in the mind. It is first suggested there, and only after it is encouraged does the possible become the probable. Always remember: If you fight off unchaste thoughts you can prevent unchaste acts.

The job of guarding your chastity is something like the job of soldiers who guard the person of the king. They are the elite corps of the army. When they do their job well, honors are heaped upon their heads. For the more important the job, the greater is the praise for doing it properly.

What about Necking?

I like the way a priest handled a question tossed at him by a high school girl in the marriage preparation course he was giving.

"Please tell me, father," she said, "how much kissing is permitted on a date?"

The priest smiled and replied:

"First you tell me—how much drinking should a couple do on a date?"

The girl thought a moment, then answered:

"As little as possible, I suppose. Or at any rate, no more than a person can handle without getting stupid."

The priest nodded.

"Exactly," he said.

Questions of necking, kissing and petting come up in almost every discussion of dating. It's always difficult to lay down hard-and-fast rules about them. There are some things in which you have to use your own good judgment, and this is one of them.

If a kiss means little more than the "hello" some people give when they greet each other, it certainly won't induce tempting thoughts. A dozen such pecks would involve no hazards—but you might feel as though you'd had a shower after they were over. On the other hand, one kiss delivered with passionate intensity might stir up feelings that had best be kept under lock and key. So the guiding rule, it seems to me, should be: "Where do we go from here?"

Another teacher once likened kissing to wine. He said that a gentle kiss might be like a sip, a longer kiss like a glassful, and a heavy, prolonged kiss like several drinks. As is well known, the more drinks the average person has had, the less he can resist the next one. This comparison means that the ability to resist sinful thoughts and desires is greatly diminished by prolonged kissing.

Most young people know that the lips are very sensitive organs, and that contact between them creates a desire for greater physical union. This fact is well recognized, because a question I'm always asked is: "How far can you go?" The answer, of course, is the one the priest gave.

As I pointed out earlier, the power of your passion is a precious gift—one that God wants you to exercise only after you're married. The vast majority of youngsters try to do what's right. Unfortunately, however, many don't realize the tremendous force of their passion. Just as you had no idea when you were six years old that you could learn algebra, say, or another language, so too you don't now realize the power of the creative urge that God has given you.

Ever Slide Down an Icy Hill?

You'll have to take the word of those older than yourself that once this passionate urge is encouraged, it's extremely difficult to stop. It's somewhat like sliding down an icy hill. Before you start to slide, you have no trouble holding your position. Slide just a bit, and you may be able to exert enough effort to stop. But take a running slide and you're gone for good. You won't be able to stop until you reach the bottom of the hill. Obviously, if you don't want to slide all the way, you've got to keep in control of the situation at the top of the hill.

Unlike the faucet (which has no feeling), passion, once aroused, is not so easily turned off. It becomes more like water in a dam that has a crack. It seeks outlet. It has a driving force of its own. And if you don't think so, then visit an obstetrician in a clinic on a busy day. As you may know, an obstetrician is a doctor who specializes in caring for women and girls who are going to have babies. You'd probably find that some of his patients are unmarried sixteen- or seventeen-year-olds. They thought they'd resist the urge to "go all the way" after they'd let themselves slide half of it. As their present condition testifies, they found that when the time came, they couldn't exercise the control they thought they had.

Two of the most distressing statistics about modern life result to a large extent from this idea of youngsters that they can control their passions. These statistics are the number of babies born to unmarried mothers and the number of marriages performed because the girl is pregnant and wants a father for her child. In recent times, there has been a shocking increase in both of these statistics.

Maybe such figures don't mean much to you. To understand their meaning clearly, just put yourself in the place of the girl who suddenly finds she's pregnant and that all of her dreams for the future have either collapsed or will have to undergo drastic changes. That education, that beautiful church wedding and reception she had dreamed about, will never look quite as rosy again.

Or put yourself in the place of the boy who stands in front of the unchangeable fact that, due to his actions, some girl is going through the emotional wringer. Maybe he will feel that marriage is the solution. But he too will have to change all his plans. Perhaps he had hoped to go to college. It will be difficult now, maybe impossible, if he has to find a job to support his unexpected family. He'll be tied down in a way he wouldn't have considered possible a few short months before.

The only safe way to control yourself is to avoid dangerous people, places and things:

People who are too fond of kissing and seem determined to go to the brink. Some day, inevitably, they'll go too far.

Places where kissing might get out of hand. Beware, for instance, of the secluded park bench and the car parked in a secluded spot.

Things which may make you less able to control yourself, such as alcohol. Even small quantities can substantially lower a teen-ager's ability to resist temptation.

When I discuss the necking problem with a group, there are usually some girls who listen attentively and agree respectfully with all of the advice given. But they obviously still have one question on their minds. Sooner or later it comes out:

"We don't get any fun out of necking, but boys expect it," they generally say. "The boys tell us they won't go out with a girl who won't neck."

That's what boys of a certain type have been saying for years, and it's just a phony sales talk. The fact is that boys want girls to hold their standards high. True, the demanding type of boy may chase a girl who's free with her caresses, but don't think for one minute that he respects her, or that he'd want his mother to meet her. He's out for all he can get.

And if he'd ditch a girl because she didn't neck, he'd also be ready to ditch her if she gave him what he wanted. And he'd be the type who'd broadcast the information and ruin her reputation in the process.

Hazards to Your Chastity

Barbara was a very bright girl about most things. She consistently got the best marks in her class and was known as a "brain." She also had very strong ideas, inherited from her mother, about the equality of the sexes. And whenever she thought that a woman was being denied the rights of a man, she could be counted upon to stand up and strike a blow for freedom.

Something had happened in her neighborhood that had her up in arms. One seventeen-year-old girl had been forced to quit school and go to another city to have a baby which had been conceived with a boy in town. While the girl had to leave under a cloud, the boy continued at high school and outwardly at least didn't have to suffer the consequences of the act in which he played such an important part.

"Why must girls always be held entirely responsible?" Barbara wanted to know. "Aren't boys equally to blame?"

Of course, the answer is that in the sight of God, the boy's sin was equally as grave as that of the poor girl who bore the physical result. It's generally a fact, however, that such things don't happen without the girl's willing cooperation, and it's true that she usually has the power to permit or prevent them from happening.

The nature of the sexes is such that a man has instincts that are easily aroused as a rule. The sight of a pretty girl, the smell of perfume, even a few softly spoken words, may cause a surge of desire within him. A kiss that to a girl may merely express affection may be to a boy a source of tempting thought.

A girl's response is a great deal more deliberate than a boy's and usually takes a much longer period of time to develop. Therefore, she has more time to take stock of any given situation. When potential danger arises, she also can act constructively while there's still time to avoid sin. Because of these factors, she's expected to exercise caution even if the boy she's with can't control himself.

I don't condone for one minute the attitude of society that says the woman is the chief culprit when a tragedy of this kind occurs. But that's how society feels about it, and—as the saying goes—"Who can fight City Hall?" Even if things are terribly unfair, girls had better realize that that's how they are and probably will continue to be.

Girls Set the Tone

A girl can control the turn of events in many ways. She can dress in such a manner that the first thought of boys who see her is not directed toward the curves of her body. She shouldn't be like the girl who "looked as though she had been forced into a dress but forgot to say when."

She can wear makeup that makes her look attractive but which is not applied with a trowel and which (rightly or wrongly, I can't say) is associated in many boys' minds with girls who are overly generous.

She can use language that says that she's a lady—not language that may entitle boys to wonder about it. One girl had developed the habit of repeating tales that would have been in bad taste in an all-boy group, let alone in mixed company. "When she told one story," one boy remarked, "I couldn't help wondering exactly how much she knew, and how much of her information she got from firsthand experience."

Girls can also set the tone of their relationship with boys because they exercise the veto power about what to do on a date. For instance, if a girl knows that a trip to the local movie house usually leads to a seat in the balcony and a two- or three-hour necking party, she'll insist upon seats in the orchestra or she'll keep away from the theater entirely. If she knows from experience that a certain type of party will lead to excessive drinking, she can turn thumbs down. And she has the power to turn aside a suggestion that she "single-date" and insist instead that she and her friend go out with another couple or two.

Lest Barbara rise to object, let me point out at once that the moral obligation of boys to avoid temptation and situations that might cause temptation is just as great as the girls'. They can offend by wearing suggestive dress, by telling off-color stories that are better left untold and that might bring a blush to a worldly sailor, and by suggesting dates that they know could lead to excessive necking, drinking, or other excesses.

There's no need to be a prude about this, no need to adopt a "holier than thou" expression. Plain common sense, combined with a sense of humor, will take care of most situations.

9. DRINKING, DRIVING AND DATES

You can do so much to have a good time on a date that it is a wonder anyone would think drinking could contribute much of value to it.

The purpose of alcohol is to make things seem a little different from what they really are. At a party of adults, drinks are served to help people relax and to take their minds off their problems, to make them less shy so that they can enjoy others' company, and so on.

Most people don't use alcohol in connection with their ordinary activities. Some may have developed the custom of taking a drink or two before meals or of drinking wine or beer with the meals, and some may take a few ounces at night to relax or to sleep more readily. It's worth noting that these reasons are legitimate and involve no question of drinking to excess.

There's no medical justification for most young people to drink. For instance, the typical teen-ager hardly needs a drink to give him an appetite. It's probably hard enough for Mom and Dad to pay his food bills as it is. He doesn't need it to sleep because he's usually off like a log the minute his head hits the pillow. And he doesn't need it to protect himself from boredom because he can have the time of his life without it.

If the truth were told, just between us, I think it would be that teen-agers who bring alcohol along on a date do it because they're trying to make like grown-ups. They no more need it—or want it for its own sake, for that matter—than they want or need a jug of catsup. But they think drinking is "the adult thing to do," so they go ahead and drink.

As you know, the Church teaches that there's nothing wrong with drinking in moderation. Wine was created, the Bible says, to make men joyful. In some Latin countries, mothers even feed wine to their three-year-olds, and nobody has ever claimed that they're trying to corrupt their children. In many wonderful Latin families particularly, boys and girls take wine with meals as a matter of course.

What does concern the Church is when drinking is done to excess. Then it becomes a sin, just as most other things done to excess (like eating) are sinful.

The Church is also concerned because drinking by youngsters can cause serious moral problems. The primary effect of alcohol is that it releases inhibitions. It keeps the mind from functioning properly and it dulls the conscience. It sometimes allows people to do things they wouldn't do in a million years if they were sober.

Exact Effects Can't Be Predicted

This effect of alcohol isn't new. It has been known since earliest times. As a result, there has always been an association between drinking to excess and immorality. The association continues today, and the danger is just as great for teenagers now as it has ever been in the past.

What makes drinking particularly dangerous on dates is that it's impossible to predict what its exact effects will be at any given time. On one occasion, a person might take two drinks and feel relaxed and cheerful. He has no desire to drink more and is at ease with the world. At another time, two drinks make him quarrelsome, ready to take offense at the slightest remarks made by others, maybe also ready to drink more than is good for him. At another time, he may feel excessively susceptible to thoughts of impurity.

These different reactions to alcohol depend upon how tired a person is, how hungry, and a host of other factors. As one man commented, "The only thing sure about the trouble caused by alcohol is that it started out to be fun."

Some youngsters hand out the line that they drink so they'll be able to "handle alcohol" and later on "drink like ladies and gentlemen." They almost act as though they're in training. From the high-minded way they talk, you almost expect them to suggest that their school principal should run around to teen-age parties looking for students who have passed out under the table, so that he can pin medals on them for doing their homework.

Maybe these youngsters are kidding themselves as well as trying to kid other people. I know of one man who deliberately chose for his son a college that had the reputation of having a greater number of lushes per square foot than any other institution in the country. This man made his choice not because the college had good teachers, but because, he said, "he wanted the boy to learn to handle alcohol like a gentleman." He changed his tune about three years later when the son decided to major in martinis and dropped all the other subjects. Maybe Papa was proud of his boy for mastering the subject, but quite a few other people were convinced that the subject had mastered the boy.

If you think about it, you'll realize that it's difficult to learn how to handle alcohol "like a lady or a gentleman" by drinking. In fact, if you want to learn how to handle alcohol, the way to do it is by *not* drinking.

Why is this so? Because the most important thing everybody has to learn about alcohol is when and how to say no. As long as you can say "No" to a drink before you make a fool of yourself, you can handle the stuff. So, more than anything, you need practice in saying "No!" to a drink.

I could tell some hair-raising stories about lives that have been ruined just because of excessive drinking on dates. I'm sure you can imagine some of these stories yourself. The story, for instance, of the sixteen-year-old girl who thought that several cocktails on a date would be the smart thing to have, who lost control of herself and her virginity as well, and who had a baby out of wedlock as a result. There's also the story of the two otherwise good kids who overindulged in beer at a party and found themselves forced to marry before either had finished high school. And the story of the girl whose reputation in her town was forever tarnished because of what happened at a party at which alcohol flowed too freely.

Another drawback to drinking on dates is that youngsters tend to emphasize it to the exclusion of everything else. In some circles, that means that the boy who can consume the most without falling over in a faint is considered the hero. As a result of such overemphasis, the usual teen-age drinking party winds up with a couple of individuals making asses of themselves and a couple of others becoming deathly sick. Since the purpose of dating is to enable persons of opposite sexes to know each other better, it's hard to see how alcohol helps in this operation. In fact, trying to develop a friendship under the influence of drink is about as far from serious preparation for marriage as you can get.

Since alcohol does nothing constructive for you except give you the false feeling that you're acting like an adult, the best advice is to handle it with as much care as you'd handle a stick of lighted dynamite. For it's just as dangerous.

The Matter of Motors

Maybe it happened. Maybe it didn't. Anyway, it makes a good story.

A physical training instructor in a big Milwaukee high school was trying to interest his class in calisthenics—push-ups, bend-overs, stoop-downs, and that sort of thing. He was getting nowhere. Finally he decided to give a pep talk.

"When you do push-ups," he said, "you strengthen your arm muscles. You can shove the gearshift into second a lot better that way.

"When you squat, you develop leg muscles. It helps you push the gas pedal harder toward the floor board.

"When you strengthen your neck muscles, you can turn

it around a lot faster. That way, you won't miss seeing any pretty girls walking down the street while you're driving.

"See? Calisthenics have a practical value after all."

The report is that the teacher had more enthusiasm shown for his exercises and better results than any other teacher had with any other class in the history of the school.

Science teachers report a similar phenomenon. Youngsters —particularly boys—may not care what happens when one part of oxygen mixes with two parts of hydrogen. But let the instructor explain how a carburetor works, and they sit at rapt attention.

I know how important an automobile is in the life of many high schoolers. Those under the legal driving age can hardly wait until it becomes lawful to sit behind the wheel. Those who own the magic paper—the operator's license—can sometimes think of little else. You've probably heard of the teenager who sat glumly in his house, moaning that he couldn't go to the corner drugstore for a soda. Someone asked whether he was being kept at home as punishment for something he'd done. "No," he said. "The car's broken."

In ninety-nine cases out of a hundred (maybe 999 out of 1000) there are no moral questions involved in driving. If you're legally qualified to drive, there's probably no good reason why you shouldn't take advantage of Detroit's ingenuity. However, you do have a moral obligation to observe all the regulations as regards speeding, stopping at red traffic lights, and the like.

Not much has been said about this, but it's a fact that the driver, young or old, who operates a vehicle recklessly might be guilty of a serious sin. Let's say a man is bulleting along at ninety miles an hour. An innocent driver pulls out from a side street. The speeding vehicle slams into it, killing the other driver. Wouldn't you say the speeder was guilty of homicide?

As you probably know, the nation's insurance companies take a pretty dim view of male drivers under twenty-five. Some families have seen their car insurance rates double or triple when a teen-ager became qualified to drive. While statistics prove that most young male drivers are just as responsible as older drivers, some lads are nuts on wheels. And the insurance companies have no way of figuring out exactly who are good drivers and who are unsafe ones. So they soak every young male alike.

The only reason I mention this is that some youngsters tend to develop a "heavy foot." They want to see what the buggy can do. I think you'd probably agree that young drivers generally are more daring and take more chances than would an older person—a parent with small children, for example, or elderly Aunt Martha when she's going to Vesper services.

You'll have to resist the tendency to speed, in the interests of safety, particularly if you're on a date or have other passengers. You can be sure your riders will get a great deal more upset over your near-misses and your speeding than you do. That seems to be common, regardless of the age of the driver.

Maybe the person at the wheel feels that he could handle the situation if an emergency arose. On the other hand, the passenger can do nothing but grind his or her teeth. At any rate, if you drive, remember that stepping on the pedal may be fun for you but torture for your companion.

It might also help to think once in a while how you'd feel if you caused an accident resulting in serious injuries or disfigurement to someone in your car. In one gruesome case, a high school senior drove his girl friend to a dance. He decided to see how much beer he could drink that night and put himself in the worst possible condition to drive home. He drove anyway. The car hit a tree, and now a once-beautiful girl carries a facial disfigurement for life. Every time the boy sees her, he realizes that he alone was the cause. So ponder these words to the wise: Alcohol and gasoline never mix. If you drink, never drive. If you drive, never drink.

What's Wrong with a Few Beers?

This rule may seem harsh to the youngster who wonders what's wrong about having a few beers at a pizza parlor at the end of an evening. He has had a few beers before, and nothing has happened. So why not this time? The answer—again—is that alcohol doesn't affect you the same way all the time. Even doctors don't understand the question thoroughly, but they know that a person may take a couple of drinks at one time and seem reasonably sober, while the same quantity of alcohol under different circumstances may make him tight. Maybe it's due to the fact that the second time, he drinks on an empty stomach, has gone a few nights without sleep, or is upset or worried.

At any rate, it's almost impossible to predict accurately what the exact effect of alcohol will be. Therefore the person who in the past has seen little effect from a few beers, may be affected in an entirely different way this time. And an accident has to happen just once to cause injury or death.

Another danger in thinking it's okay to have a few drinks while driving: Let's say the driver manages okay on three beers this time. The next time he'll be inclined to think he can get away with four. He'll keep experimenting until he's plastered when he sits behind the wheel.

And another danger: When drivers stop off for a drink, there's a strong chance that they won't limit themselves to the number they expected. In fact, I think the nation's bars would go out of business if they sold only the number of drinks patrons expected to buy when they walked into the place. What usually happens is that people get a couple, are having a good time, and then hate to leave. So there's a tendency to have more than they really intended to have. Thus the risk that a driver will leave the place in an unfit condition to operate a car. (Of course, anybody who found himself in that condition should leave the car where it's parked and walk home, or let a sober person do the driving. Alas, not many people are wise enough to do this. Under the influence, they think they could pilot a transatlantic jet liner without trouble.)

The other moral hazard results not when the car is in motion, but when it's parked. It has been said that more virtue has been lost in the nation's "lovers' lanes" than in any other place.

Usually the loss of virginity, reputation and the state of grace is not the result of deliberate planning. Often it just happens when a car is parked in a secluded spot and neither the boy nor girl can stop their necking when it gets out of hand.

The best way to avoid this calamity is to avoid parking in secluded spots where temptation lurks. A good precaution is to plan in advance what to do on your dates and to plan your going and coming so that no time is left for such activities. Let's say a girl must be home at eleven-thirty. If she leaves the dance at eleven-fifteen, there'll be no time for "lovers' lane" parking.

10. THE IMPORTANCE OF YOUR REPUTATION

If I had only a few sentences to describe a girl I'll call Kathy, I'd say she was the type who never listens to advice from other people but must always learn the hard way. Her parents and teachers could tell her something from morning till night, but she'd never believe it unless and until she found it out for herself.

Now, you can put it down as a rule that anybody who can't take advice from his elders is headed for trouble. The whole purpose of advice, when given by your parents and teachers, is to point out the possible mistakes that lie ahead in life and how to avoid making them. If you won't take advice, you'll make mistakes—it's as simple as that. And the mistakes may seriously affect your whole life.

Kathy just refused to accept the word of her parents that a good reputation is one of the most precious possessions anyone can have. If she heard that statement once, she probably heard it a dozen times—and from as many different sources. But she always took the attitude that her parents and teachers were trying to put something over on her. So she refused to believe it.

When Kathy was a sophomore, a boy invited her to a school dance. After the dance, he parked the car in a secluded spot and began to neck. Kathy was all too willing to let him. If she thought at all about all the advice she had heard about the dangers of such action, she gave no evidence of it. Their necking led to intercourse.

The next day Kathy had regrets, but she soothed her guilt feelings by telling herself that only she and the boy were involved and that no one else would know. A few weeks later, another boy invited her to another dance. The same thing happened afterward.

A week later, another boy called, then another and another. Soon Kathy's phone was ringing day and night. But the boys who called were types she wouldn't ordinarily date—"creeps," in her term, who obviously were interested only in having intercourse with her.

What had been happening did not fully dawn on her until she discovered that none of her girl friends wanted to be seen with her, and that boys of a certain type began to make obscene remarks whenever she passed by. Within the short period of a month or so, she had literally ruined her reputation. She had thought that the boys would keep it a secret that they had committed a sin with her. This notion is absolutely false. More often than not, a boy who seduces a girl can hardly wait until he can announce the sordid fact to everyone he knows. And they in turn will do all they can to spread the news all over town.

That is precisely what happened in Kathy's case. The first boy told his friends what had happened, and one of them decided to try her too. When he succeeded, he told everyone he knew. Soon every undesirable boy in town knew Kathy was "available." But no decent boy, looking for a girl friend he could introduce to his parents, would give her a second thought.

Reputation Is Worth More than Gold

What is reputation? It is society's estimate of our character—in other words, what people think of us. A good reputation is of great importance. We all want other people to think highly of us. We want them to respect us as persons and to approve what we do.

This public opinion is surprisingly accurate. If most of your classmates think a certain girl is wild, for example, you can be sure she has given them reasons to think so. Such ideas are not pulled out of a hat.

There are many ways to maintain a good reputation—or to acquire a bad one. You know, of course, all of us are judged by the friends we have. If they are the low type, we cannot help but be put in their category. But if they behave as they should, we will also be highly regarded.

Another way is by how you talk. Teen-agers sometimes like to take the opposite side of an argument. For example, in class one day a teacher spoke about all the trouble that excessive drinking could cause. Just to shock the teacher, one boy decided to argue that drinking was within the rights of a teen-ager, and that the school should permit hard liquor at the junior prom. Another time, the same boy argued that the principal had no right to prohibit necking by pupils on the school grounds. This boy may have been saying these things just to create excitement, but other pupils could not be blamed for thinking he had several loose screws.

We're all also judged by how we dress. "Clothes make the man," the saying goes. And whether you think things should be this way or not, that's how it is. You could look at a boy or girl, I'm sure, and come up with a fairly accurate appraisal of what he or she is like—the kind of crowd he or she runs around with, the things that he or she thinks it's okay to do, and so on. Other people can size you up the same way.

One girl had quite a shock learning this simple fact. As a high school sophomore, she decided to go all out to get the boys to turn around and look when she strolled by. She put on false eyelashes, tight sweater, tight slacks, and shoes with skyscraper heels. She let her hair hang down over her face, the way beatniks are supposed to do in Greenwich Village. Then she pasted lipstick, nail polish and toenail polish all over.

It probably took her a couple of hours to get into this apparatus every day, but it had the effect she thought she wanted. Whenever she walked out of the house, people turned to stare. Boys whistled. Those riding in cars stuck their heads out the windows and honked their horns. She was getting noticed, all right.

Then one day she walked into a classroom by way of the back door and overheard a couple of boys talking about her. I wouldn't repeat what they said. You can imagine. She went home, took off the false eyelashes and the rest of the junk, and threw them into the garbage pail.

Manners Protect Morals

Suppose you happened to be walking in the most disreputable section of your town and chanced to peep into a cheap, dirty saloon. You see a woman at the bar, one foot perched on the brass rail. She is wearing an extreme hairdo, and the color of her hair—a violent yellow—is certainly not the color she was born with. She is wearing a heavy application of rouge and facial powder and has applied mascara around her eyes with the skill of an apprentice painter wielding an eight-inch brush. A cigarette dangles from her lips when she is not tossing off swigs of whiskey like a stevedore. When she addresses herself to the bartender, there are profanities in every sentence.

What sort of person would you say that woman is? The type you'd like as a mother? Would you like to marry someone like her and introduce her to your own parents as the future mother of your children?

Of course not. You'd have an idea of the state of that woman's morals. Chances are that your idea would be right. Yet—and this is a point worth remembering—this woman has not done anything morally wrong. Good women wear makeup. They smoke. Some use profane (not blasphemous) expressions. Some drink—a few, perhaps, drink a bit more at times than they should.

But the total impression that this woman's manners convey is not that of a "good woman." Her ways of acting strongly suggest that she is a person of loose morals.

Which sounds the theme of this section: That your manners protect your morals, and that the way you act is indicative of the type of person you are. If you want to safeguard your morals, therefore, guard your manners.

Youngsters generally don't get into serious trouble suddenly. Rather, they've been showing an increasing indifference to their manners long before. Only after their manners break down do their morals break down too.

For example, one girl decided that she'd be "unconventional." She walked around the streets barefoot. She smoked cigarettes from long holders. She refused to bathe regularly. She decided to talk with men on an equal footing—using the same expressions they used for the coarsest human functions.

Soon she met a man who took one look at her and decided that if she was so unconventional in her manners, chances were that she was also unconventional in her morals. She got herself involved in a mess simply because her manners had conveyed the impression that she was an easy mark.

Teachers have long known that the way you dress and the way you carry yourself are indications of the way you think. They expect you to come to school neatly and properly dressed, because they know that you then will be in a better position to absorb the knowledge they have to offer. On the other hand, if pupils were allowed to come to school dressed in shorts or dirty dungarees, without washing themselves, combing their hair, cleaning their fingernails, or making any effort at a presentable appearance, they certainly wouldn't have a suitable mental attitude toward learning. In fact, experienced teachers often can spot the potential trouble makers in a class by looking them over the first few days of the year. Those who come properly dressed and behave as though they want to learn, invariably make better students than the unwashed, ill-dressed individuals who slouch with an indifferent look as the teacher begins to teach.

Take the matter of smoking. Now most adults smoke, and some of them started in their late teens. Considering what we now know about the harm done by smoking to their heart and lungs, all older folks would be better off today if they had not started smoking at all. I am not concerned, here, however, with your future health. But I am interested in what smoking, particularly in your early teens, might mean. Are you trying to be a "big shot"? Is this your way of letting your friends know you don't care about the wishes of your parents? Are you developing sneaky habits? Does smoking mean that you are running too far too fast and with the wrong pack? You will have to make your own decisions, but sometimes it's little things like this that reveal a lot about the real you.

Don't get me wrong. God never said you have to wear a clean shirt or be a nonsmoker in order to get to heaven. But it certainly makes sense to think that the person who wears the clean shirt shows a much more favorable attitude.

What does all this mean as far as dating is concerned? It means this: When you associate with the opposite sex, if you yourself maintain—and insist that the other person maintain—a proper level of decorum, you are going to be that much further away from temptation and the possibilities of trouble.

Say a boy dates a girl. He appears at her home clean and well dressed. He stands when she enters a room, opens the door for her when she passes through, shows respect for her mother and father, uses proper language when talking to her. He displays by his actions that he's anxious to do the right thing, and it may be safe to assume that he will show his desire to do the right thing in all of his relationships with the girl.

Or say a girl insists that such simple courtesies be shown to her. She lets the boy know that she won't tolerate dirty jokes or dirty language. She insists upon being "treated like a lady" in minor matters. She'll certainly be in a stronger position, therefore, to insist that she be "treated like a lady" in the most important matter of all.

During the summer, I spend a little time at a beach on the

Atlantic Ocean. On any given day, dozens of high school boys and girls can be seen on the beaches. From the way they act there, I think you can get a reasonably accurate picture of their standards. Not long ago, two lasses showed up in highly revealing bathing suits, and acted in a way to induce tempting thoughts on the part of boys. Lying around on the beach, they allowed themselves to be pawed (in some cases, even doing the pawing). From the way they threw beer cans around and used the Lord's name in vain, it didn't take a detective to deduce that these girls showed no respect for themselves and therefore invited no respect from others.

Other boys and girls on the beach are obviously there for a good, clean time. They may be listening to music, playing cards or other games, carrying on conversations in quiet tones, using language that they wouldn't be afraid to have overheard in the living room. In general, they're giving a clear indication by their manners that they're striving to lead moral lives.

The conclusion's obvious. Do you want others to have a high regard for you? Then have a high regard for yourself. Think of yourself as a person with a good reputation—one who observes the rules of the game, who does nothing to be ashamed of, who gives other people no reason to question his good name.

If you have a good image of yourself and live up to it, others will come to think of you as you think of yourself. Because if you have a high regard for your own reputation, you will find it unthinkable to do things that will damage it.

Remember always: Your good reputation is one of your greatest possessions. Whether you keep it or lose it will be up to you alone. But if you should lose it, you may have to spend a lifetime trying to regain it.

11. GOING STEADY

As long as you date in groups and don't pair off, you won't have to consider the question of going steady. Of course, there is nothing wrong with going steady at the right time. In fact, it is necessary for engaged couples and probably even for those who could entertain the idea of marriage if the subject came up. But like everything that is good in one place, it may also be bad in another place.

Just to keep the record straight, let me define what we mean by "going steady." I would call this the "exclusive commitment of a boy and a girl to each other for a long time." And going steady is *wrong* when the boy and girl have no hope or prospects of marriage in the reasonable future. I would say the reasonable future is within a couple of years at most.

Strictly speaking, therefore, you shouldn't begin to think of going steady until you are ready to think of marriage. At that time, your formal schooling will be nearly at an end, and you will be able to accept the responsibilities of the married state. That is why going steady is a little absurd for someone who is just entering his teens.

This idea of going steady has reached ridiculous extremes. A nine-year-old girl once stopped me on the street to ask, "Is it a sin for me to go steady?" Another eleven-year-old girl reported that a friend of hers had gone steady with three boys in her class already.

In another case (all too typical, I fear) a boy of sixteen, a high school sophomore, dates three nights a week with a girl of fourteen. Another sixteen-year-old boy spends every evening at the home of a girl in his class. They go out together every Saturday night and often spend their Sundays together as well. They are actually together more hours of the week than the girl's mother and father and the boy's mother and father combined.

Well, you may ask, what's wrong with that?

First of all, of course, it's obvious that a boy and girl who are in each other's company for such long periods of time are more likely to take liberties with each other. The boys and girls in the two cases cited above, might therefore be considered frequenting an approximate occasion of sin. If they continued to see so much of each other alone for a long period of time, a real mortal sin would be involved.

Another reason we object to going steady is that it keeps a boy and girl from meeting others of the opposite sex, from getting to know more about boys and girls generally and from being able to decide which characteristics to look for in a marriage partner.

Suppose a girl enters a dress shop. The clerk shows only one dress and tells the girl that's all the choice there is. The would-be buyer would stalk off in a rage. She wants to see dozens of dresses, to look at their labels, to see how they are designed, to try them on, before she makes her choice. Yet the same girl will "go steady" at fifteen and make a total commitment to a boy without taking advantage of the opportunity of getting to know boys from among whom a more intelligent choice of a married partner could be made.

I realize that there are many reasons why boys and girls seek steady companions of the opposite sex. For one thing, it seems to be the thing to do—like listening to the latest records and keeping tabs on the top tunes of the week. But it also seems to stem from the mistaken idea that the girl of fifteen without a boy friend is somehow doomed to spinsterhood for life, and that a boy without a steady girl friend lacks appeal to the opposite sex.

If you asked all the youngsters who go steady what their real reasons are, you would find that very few are truly attracted to their boy friends or girl friends. They do it so that they can say they have a "steady," in order to make sure that

they won't be out in the cold when a big dance or other social events come along. Their real reasons, therefore, are not
related to the personalities or characters of the boys or girls
they go steady with. They like the idea of going steady more
than they like the person they go with.

A youngster may think that the advantages of going steady
outweigh all the disadvantages, and that priests, parents and
teachers who object to it are all out of touch with the times.
If you think that, you will have to realize that these persons
with far greater experience than your own can look at the
entire picture. They can trace many disasters—premature marriages, lost reputations, and similar tragedies—to this idea of
going steady too young. Older people also know that when
you go steady too young, you miss the opportunity to develop
your full character as a man or woman.

On the other hand, just by keeping free from "entangling al-
liances," you can do much to make sure that you'll make a
happy marriage and lead a happy life. If you wait awhile,
you'll be older, wiser and much better able to decide whether
a boy or girl is the person you would want to hook up with
for forty or fifty years. Probably you'll also have a clearer idea
of what you want to do with your life, and you'll be able to
decide whether a certain boy or girl would help or hinder you
in doing this. And you'll be making it easier to get all the
education you'll need to help you make full use in your life
of the talents God has given you.

I've mentioned the importance of education before, and
I'm sure you've heard much on this subject from your parents and teachers. But the facts stare us all in the face and
are so important that I will repeat them at the risk of being
monotonous. In fact, a group of prominent economists have
just concluded that millions of people will continue to be un-
employed every year in the United States from now on, all
as a result of the introduction of laborsaving machinery I
mentioned earlier. "Going steady" too early can put a lad on
the unemployment line of the future, just because it leads him

to get married and to discontinue his schooling long before he is really prepared to hold a regular job.

When you come right down to it, you have no choice about going steady in your early years in high school. Because of the hazards involved, the Church teaches that you must not go steady until you are ready to marry. If you are not ready to marry, you cannot have the privileges of those older than yourself, any more than an eight-year-old, for example, is entitled to the privilege of smoking.

12.   WHEN IS IT REALLY LOVE?

We have talked about qualities you should look for in a mate—unselfishness, idealism, willingness to listen to the other's point of view, willingness to accept the responsibilities of parenthood, and so on. But put all these qualities together and you'll need one more ingredient to make your marriage click.

What is this mysterious thing? I'll give you a clue. Poets write of it, songwriters sing of it, storytellers devote all their time (it seems) to it. It's love.

In our scientific age, we have been able to measure the qualities that successfully married people have. We know that a man and woman from the same social, educational and economic background, with the same religion and similar ideas about what marriage should consist of, have a better chance of making a go of it than the man and woman who hold utterly different ideas about life. But even if you take two persons as alike as cars on an assembly line, they probably will not be truly united in marriage unless a strong emotional and physical attraction exists between them.

Many persons have tried to define what that attraction is. They usually wind up working the word "mystery" into the definitions, indicating that they really don't know the answer. It's an elusive thing and either the attraction exists or it doesn't.

But in addition to all the good, solid virtues you should seek in a dating and mating partner, you ought to make sure that his or her presence brings a glow to your heart, that you would rather be with him or her than anyone else, and that he or she inspires you with the confidence that together you can answer the emotional problems that will inevitably come your way. When there is a meeting of hearts, there is also a deep desire to understand the other partner, a desire to co-operate, an urge to do what is best for him or her.

Is such an attraction the all-important ingredient in marriage? That is a good question which young people often ask. It certainly can be a powerful cementing force, a means of making two persons truly "one in mind, heart and soul."

On the other hand, I don't think you can accurately describe it as "love." For love rarely exists at the beginning of a marriage. All that a couple have when they march to the altar is the *beginning* of love. There may be a strong sexual attraction between them, a strong desire for one to be with the other, a strong sense of compatibility. But there cannot be a truly deep sense of love. That is something that will develop over many years and will be the result of day-to-day consideration, courtesy and self-sacrifice—the regular denial of one's selfish interests for the benefit of the other.

That's why it's important to understand that a strong physical and emotional attraction, *by itself,* will not be enough to make a successful marriage. Consider this: Many thousands of divorces are granted in this country every year. If you were to ask the ex-husbands and wives whether they were in love when they married, they would almost invariably answer:

"Well, I thought I was, but—"

Obviously only two things could have happened: Either they did not know what true love was, or if it was love, it was not strong enough to hold them together when the inevitable storms of married life arose. They may have expected too much from the attraction they felt for each other and not enough from the other necessary qualities—unselfishness, sense of responsibility, willingness to live up to the rules and regulations of marriage.

Young people have a very strong sexual urge, and therefore may feel a powerful attraction for another person that is based upon this physical factor alone. But after a few years, the sexual urge as a magnetic force begins to weaken. When that happens, a marriage based on physical attraction alone has nothing to hold it together.

What Hollywood Teaches about "Love"

You can see vivid proof of this fact in Hollywood. In the movie capital of the world can probably be found the best-looking women in the world. They certainly are more alluring than the average woman you'd see in your neighborhood supermarket. But the movie starlet marries—and is very likely to get divorced after a few years. The woman you see in the supermarket marries—and makes a success of it. Explanation? The starlet's marriage was based on physical attraction alone. The other woman's marriage had a great deal more to support it.

Since the Family Life Bureau of the New York Archdiocese has been sponsoring the annual ceremony at St. Patrick's Cathedral at which His Eminence, the Cardinal, distributes handsomely engraved certificates to couples celebrating their fiftieth wedding anniversaries, I've had many chances to observe how beautiful Christian married love can really be.

Every year the husbands and wives, with their children and grandchildren, pack the Cathedral to overflowing. But among all the couples, I've seen few women who would have won beauty prizes in their youth and few men who would have been signed up to play a leading man's role in Hollywood. What I mean is that these wonderful people who have successfully lived together for fifty years are—even as you and I —ordinary people without any great physical distinction that sets them apart.

But here they are—still in love with each other, perhaps even more in love than ever before. The power of their passion has left them now, but what they have is a beautiful spirit of the soul. Goodness of heart they have in abundance, and it's this quality—not any strong physical attraction they may have had

—which has enabled them to lead truly successful, truly Christian lives.

To sum up: The very best chance for a long and successful marriage exists when a boy and girl have high ideals in common, when their backgrounds are sufficiently alike so that they regard the objectives of life in much the same way, when they have the same interests and attitudes—and when they feel a "mysterious," yet very definite attraction, between each other. The attraction should be spiritual, as well as emotional and physical.

When this attraction exists, along with the other necessary qualities I have mentioned, you can be sure that you are giving yourself the greatest possible chance of developing the unity of soul, mind and heart that is the basis of true love.

Beware of Imitations!

Mary Ann, who is twenty-three, married and the mother of two small boys, is talking:

"I just saw my old friend Tom as I was walking down the street. I haven't seen him since he went into the army six years ago, and I couldn't believe my eyes. Could this be the boy I almost married when I was seventeen?

"It seemed like real love then. Tom was the first boy I ever dated and I thought it was the real thing. When he went into the army, he wanted me to marry him right away, but my parents persuaded me to wait. Soon after that I met Jim, and I began to wonder what I ever saw in Tom. Seeing him again makes me realize what a terrible mistake it would have been to elope with him. Now, he's not my idea of a good marriage prospect at all. I must have been out of my mind to consider marrying him for one instant."

Mary Ann's experience is not unusual. At seventeen, she obviously was not in love with Tom. But she had a severe case of being "in love with love."

Having a boy friend was a new experience. It was strange and wonderful to hear how pretty she was, to have him listen to each word from her lips as though it were filled with the wisdom of the ages, to be treated like a newly crowned Queen of England.

For the first time, she also was experiencing new emotional depths. Never before had she known the sensation of being able to feel so intensely about someone of the opposite sex, and in such a way which she never felt for her parents, brothers or sisters. If truth be told, she was not so much "in love" with Tom as with the idea that she could feel that way about anyone.

This novelty of love is quite a usual thing. Most people who date experience it. For a time, they are convinced that the individual who provokes that feeling in them is the one they will love forever. They do not realize that Tom, Dick or Harry, or Edna, Betty or Claire also could provoke the same feeling. This stage is known as infatuation, and also as "puppy love."

In a way, it's a pleasant state of affairs. It's generally harmless. It may last a few weeks, possibly as long as a summer. Here's a typical case:

A boy and girl met in July at a summer colony. They became madly attached to each other. They wondered how they ever lived without each other in the past or ever could live without each other in the future. Then came September. He went to his home, 150 miles away from hers, and faithfully promised to write every day. But with the first frost of Autumn the romance faded. All that remained was a memory that quickly dimmed. When they met again two years later, they barely recognized each other.

Don't get me wrong. The process of being "in love with love" is a natural process of growing up. There is really nothing wrong with it, unless, of course, it is permitted to get out-of-hand morally. This is not likely to happen, however, if a boy and girl bring the normal ideals of boyhood or girlhood to their relationship.

When Is It the "Real Thing"?

The danger lies in mistaking infatuation for true love. Sometimes the feeling they have for each other becomes so great that the young people are tempted to throw over all their plans for a lifetime in order to savor it to the fullest. As Mary Ann's friend suggested, they are tempted to quit school, elope, or do something else equally drastic.

They usually live to regret their impulsiveness. A young fellow of twenty-two now is stuck with an unhappy marriage and a job he detests—one without any prospects for advancement and without any real challenge to his abilities—because he thought an infatuation five years ago was the genuine thing. He had been getting excellent marks in high school and could look forward confidently to a good career as an engineer. Then he met a girl, fell "in love with love," and ran off with her.

Now he can clearly see that the girl was not the best choice he could have made, by any means. But he has two children to support and he can only shake his head sadly and try to make the best of the situation.

Marriages between "first loves" have worked out well, of course. But their chances of doing so are much less than those between young men and women who have had a real opportunity to consider carefully what qualities they are looking for in a mate.

Infatuated youngsters sometimes fail to think of what is involved in marriage and of all the responsibilities that must be met, but are swept away by the great romance of the moment. And they overlook the fact that marriage must stand up not only during the days of young love, but also during the many different phases through which husbands and wives pass as they travel down the road of life.

Infatuation often goes hand in hand with the lack of any

realistic idea of what marriage is like. Often, therefore, there's no relationship to the real thing. Many people unfortunately believe what they read in the gooey novels often found in women's magazines or what they see in the movies or on television. That's the story in which boy meets girl and—just like that—they live happily ever after. If you believe this sort of thing, I'm sorry to say, you'll have a rough adjustment to make when the true facts of life catch up with you.

Many a girl seems to think marriage is just a long, legalized necking session. That her husband will whisper sweet nothings into her ear at all hours of the day and night. That through some magic they'll be able to agree on all the problems of life with nary a cross word between them. That in their snug wedded bliss, the ordinary problems of life will not bother them.

This girl has never seen a marriage even remotely like this (certainly not in her own home, for example) but she disregards this little item because her marriage is going to be "different." So she suffers quite a shock when hubby comes home at night, gives her a somewhat absentminded kiss, and then settles down behind the TV screen all evening. Of course, he should be more considerate, because a woman who spends all her time in the home alone or with little children certainly deserves companionship at night. But the truth is that it is extremely unlikely that a husband will continue to treat his wife as he did on their wedding day.

You've heard that expression, "The honeymoon's over." It has become so popular because it means something. It means that anybody who marries can expect his or her partner to let down the hair a bit, to relax now that the chase is over, and to settle down to a way of living that will be more comfortable over the long span of years.

So before you fully convince yourself that your first love is the great, lasting heartthrob of your life, try to remember that it may be just a temporary experience.

Nor need you feel that your life has been ruined and

your future permanently darkened if—as usually happens—the bright glitter of infatuation falls away and you go back to living, much as you did before.

A true feeling between a man and woman must stand the tests of time. Before you are willing to bank that your sense of love will carry you through a lifetime in marriage, you should be willing to put it to that test.

13. HOW LONG SHOULD A COURTSHIP BE?

If you could believe the ads you see on television, in newspapers, magazines and elsewhere, you probably would conclude that the best way to be a success in romance is to use a certain toothpaste, a particular hairgrease, or a special body deodorant. Probably all these things help to make you more attractive physically and therefore more desirable as a marriage partner. So maybe no great harm is done by the wild claims that manufacturers of such products sometimes make.

A few years ago, however, one company ran a widespread series of ads congratulating engaged girls on hooking a man. The ads implied that it was all done with a brand of soap. I don't mind the implied claim that soap is all a girl needs to be attractive to a boy, because the claim is so ridiculous that no one takes it seriously. But I do object to the idea that getting engaged should be the cause for a great flow of congratulations.

The truth is that becoming engaged is the beginning of a deadly serious piece of business—in fact, perhaps the most serious business you will engage in in your lifetime. It is not the end of a successful chase, but rather the beginning of a prayerful search. For during this engagement period, you must settle down to the hard task of determining once and for all whether this is the person you want to be married to until death.

How long should courtship be? To this question there seems to be only one logical answer: "As long as necessary to make you reasonably sure that you could or could not lead a happy and holy life as this person's partner." If you decide yes, you are ready for the altar. If you decide no, you should break off the friendship.

The key word there is reasonably. I doubt that you could be

reasonably certain about such an important thing if you know someone only for a month or two. On the other hand, I would guess that you were supercautious if your engagement ran on for several years.

An engagement of a couple of months generally is too short to enable you to learn as much as you should about your expected partner. There is a strong danger that you will rush into a situation for which you have not been fully prepared. The expression, "Marry in haste and repent in leisure," has come down through the years as a warning from generation to generation that quick marriages lead to quick problems.

We have a large-scale example of this fact in the marriage records during World War II. Servicemen and their girls feared that the man would be sent away at once and might not return for months or years. There was a rash of two-week engagements. The results? In 1946—when the war was over and husbands and wives had had a chance to consider what they had done—more divorces were granted than in any other year in history.

The Short and Long of Engagements

If your engagement is too short, you will not get to know the character defects and good qualities of your prospective mate. You will be unable to find out whether your intended partner has deep-seated convictions about various aspects of life—the importance of children and family life, what sacrifices should be made for career or social ambitions, and so on. You will not get to know your intended's family as well as you should. True, you will marry a man or woman and not the whole family, but you would be surprised at the part in-laws play in the lives of many married couples. In fact, adjusting to in-laws is one of the greatest problems newlyweds face in the first year of marriage.

A courtship that drags on over several years has many undesirable aspects too. A man and woman who are engaged for a long time tend to lose some of the newness and spontaneity they had earlier, and some of the glamor and mystery that attracted them to each other, too.

When a courtship is prolonged, there is also a danger that the couple will resort to sins of impurity. A man and woman who see much of each other for a number of months may not find it difficult to practice chastity, because they know that their marriage will not be far off and that they then will be permitted to express fully their love for each other. Chastity becomes more difficult if the marriage is years away.

Incidentally, an engaged couple have no more "rights" than a boy or girl who have just met. The idea that they can take liberties with each other is completely false. If anything, they now should be more circumspect than ever, because they are preparing to receive the great sacrament of Matrimony.

A final reason I don't like the soapmaker's notion that an engagement is "Endsville" rather than a beginning, is that it may cause an engaged couple to think that they are obliged to go through with the marriage. Nothing could be further than the truth. Inasmuch as an engagement is a time when two persons make a thorough investigation of each other's qualities, it stands to reason that either should be free to call off the marriage if he or she is not satisfied with what an investigation turns up.

If this weren't so, there really wouldn't be any point to an engagement at all.

At the pre-Cana Conferences that we sponsor for engaged couples—meetings where they discuss questions with a priest and a doctor about marriage—I always remark that our work won't be a true success unless we help some man and woman to decide that they're not really made for each other, and that their chances for happiness would be greater with other partners. That may sound harsh, but it's true.

The surprising thing is that people who break off engagements generally go on to meet partners with whom they make a good adjustment and lead happy lives. Recently a young woman broke off an engagement with a boy she had known for years from the same neighborhood. There was a little flurry of excitement at the time because the invitations had all been printed, the hall had been arranged for, and all the other details for the inevitable wedding party were in the works. The engagement was broken, however, and the girl soon met another man at the office where she was working. They wooed and wed. Meanwhile, the boy met another girl and married her. Not long ago the two couples met. Both the former bride-to-be and former bridegroom-to-be left the meeting thanking their luck in breaking off the engagement when they did. Both were convinced that they are much better off with their present spouses.

Please don't get the idea that I mean to imply that anybody who breaks off an engagement is certain to be glad of it. But there are countless cases to prove that a broken engagement is not necessarily a lifetime tragedy. So remember that you need never be ashamed about breaking off an engagement, even if you do it on your wedding day. Of course, it would cause some embarrassment if you did it then. But the embarrassment would pass. The agony of a bad marriage, on the other hand, would remain for your lifetime.

Watch Out for Warning Signs

Every priest doing parish work for any length of time has met husbands and wives who were having trouble with their marriage. And in most cases, the husbands and wives had been having trouble for months—if not years—before they sought the help of the priest.

When the priest asks a few questions, he generally learns that the *root* of the trouble goes back not a few months, nor even a few years. Rather, it often goes back to before the couple were even married. The difficulty often could have been clearly foreseen by a man or woman almost from the beginning of their engagement. "Coming events cast their shadows before them." And the man or woman who is going to be a difficult marriage partner gives many warnings long in advance.

Of course, priests and other marriage counselors have had much experience in observing happy and unhappy marriages (or well-adjusted and maladjusted marriages). They can readily list the main causes and character deficiencies that lead a couple into trouble. So if you want to make a good marriage, and to avoid difficulty five, ten or twenty years after the ceremony, pay attention to this list. And think twice before dating, going steady with, or becoming engaged to, any of the following types:

The moody, won't-talk type. The boy or girl who retreats into a shell and won't tell you what's on his mind—the sulker, the pouter, the lad or lass who inflicts long periods of silence upon you rather than discuss his or her gripes in a calm, reasonable fashion—beware of such a person! He or she is likely to be difficult to deal with. True, we all have moody periods, times when we would rather keep to ourselves. But the person who does it habitually will find it difficult to communicate with you later on, and mutual problems will be impossible to solve in a way satisfactory to you both.

The person who goes to emotional extremes. Everybody "blows his top" once in a while, feels elated or depressed, or has emotional experiences occasionally. After all, we're not a bunch of stones. But it's also necessary to keep some control over our emotions. Because if we let them run wild, they can well overwhelm us.

A boy or girl who's so quick on the trigger that he or she's ready for a fight at the slightest imagined insult is going to be mighty difficult to deal with. So is the touchy person, with feelings so sensitive that they pain at the slightest suggestion of criticism. And so too is the person who's a little too ready to indulge in self-pity, jealousy, and envy.

When a person habitually loses control over his or her emotions, that person's mental health may well be in danger. And so may the mental health of people who have to live close to this boiling-pot.

The excessive drinker. A boy or girl who thinks any social event is incomplete without a few drinks may be developing a terribly dangerous habit. Statistics show that one in every dozen individuals will become an alcoholic—one whose life is made unmanageable by drink, and who finds it difficult to be a normally decent, responsible husband or wife. This figure is terrifying and it certainly proves that the person who gets caught in the drink habit is playing a game of Russian roulette not only with himself but also with his family.

Youngsters sometimes think that alcoholics somehow wish their conditions upon themselves. The fact is that almost every alcoholic once was sure that "it could never happen" to him.

The excessive gambler. A weary wife once remarked that young people get plenty of warnings to beware of a marriage partner who drinks too much, but that she'd rather have a drinking husband than a gambling one. This may be only one person's opinion, but there's no doubt that the gambling habit can be a killer once it takes hold. There are people who are lost without their daily racing sheet with the lineup of horses for the day's races—as lost as is the alcoholic without his drink. And the consequences are often the same. The compulsive gambler neglects his family and madly throws away money desperately needed to support his wife and children. Although he often realizes that he's making an ass of himself, he often can't seem to be able to shake the habit.

The person who lacks responsibility. Some teen-agers are the life of the party—great fun to be with. Nothing wrong with that! In fact, more power to them. We need bright lights for dark paths. But no life can be lived on good times alone. Everybody has to shoulder responsibility.

Consider the student who is always out for a good time.

He seriously neglects his studies and will never give a hand to help around the house because it interferes with his pleasure. What will he be like in fifteen years? What choice will he make when he's expected to be at work but his friends keep urging him to take the day off to go to a ball game or take a fishing trip? If he has not learned to accept obligations little by little as he has grown up, he will not be ready to accept them as a married man. So the irresponsible boy of sixteen is not likely to be greatly responsible at twenty-five.

The boy or girl who needs constant excitement. Some people seem to have nervous systems that require them to be on the go all of the time. They never want to sit still, relax, and enjoy a few calm hours. These always-on-the-go people find it hard to settle down after marriage and spend a quiet evening at home. If they need constant excitement, they will not find it in marriage. And there's a strong possibility that they will begin to look for it outside.

Someone with a strong streak of selfishness. I hope I am not beating this point to death, but from what I have seen, I would say that a selfish person is the worst possible marital risk. The reason is that selfishness usually underlies most of the other troubles that arise. For example:

The irresponsible person is selfish because he cares so much about his own pleasures that he's unwilling to fulfill his obligations to others. The person who won't communicate is so eager to satisfy his own ego that he won't give other people their due. The chronic seeker after thrills is so determined to satisfy his own wishes that he does not care much about others.

A very selfish person will not make the sacrifices that *must* be made if a marriage is to succeed. He will not curtail his desires for the sake of his wife or children. He will always want his own way—or else. Wrap yourself up with such a person and you can resign yourself to becoming a slave, or of constantly having to fight for your basic rights.

The Promise You Make at Marriage

Right here, let me quote the instruction before marriage that the priest reads as the bride and groom stand before him at the altar:

"Dear friends in Christ: As you know, you are about to enter a union which is most sacred and most serious, most sacred because established by God Himself, most serious because it will bind you together for life in a relationship so close and so intimate that it will profoundly influence your whole future. That future, with its hopes and disappointments, its successes and its failures, its pleasures and its pains, its joys and its sorrows, is hidden from your eyes. You know that these elements are mingled in every life, and are to be expected in your own. And so, not knowing what is before you, you take each other for better or for worse, for richer or poorer, in sickness and in health, until death.

"Truly, then, these words are most serious. It is a beautiful tribute to your undoubted faith in each other, that recognizing their full import, you are nevertheless so willing and ready to pronounce them. And because these words involve such solemn obligations, it is most fitting that you rest the security of your wedded life upon the great principle of self-sacrifice. And so you begin your married life by the voluntary and complete surrender of your individual lives in the interest of that deeper and wider life which you are to have in common. Henceforth you belong entirely to each other; you will be one in mind, one in heart, and one in affections. And whatever sacrifices you may hereafter be required to make to preserve this common life, always make them generously. Sacrifice is usually difficult and irksome. Only love can make it easy; and perfect love can make it a joy.

"We are willing to give in proportion as we love. And when love is perfect, the sacrifice is complete. God so loved the world that He gave His only begotten Son; and the Son so loved us that He gave Himself for our salvation. 'Greater love than this no man hath, that a man lay down his life for his friends.'

"No greater blessing can come to your married life than pure conjugal love, loyal and true to the end. May, then, this love with which you join your hands and hearts today, never fail, but grow deeper and stronger as the years go on. And if true love and the unselfish spirit of perfect sacrifice guide your every action, you can expect the greatest measure of earthly happiness that may be allotted to man in this vale of tears."

If the Church puts so much stress on the importance of unselfishness at that sacred moment, you can be sure that she knows what she's doing. She has seen millions of marriages down through the centuries and she has the experience to know that this one characteristic can often make or break the marriage.

I'm thinking of a man and woman who were in the pink of health when they were married. But just a few years later, the wife was stricken with infantile paralysis and forced to spend the rest of her life in a wheelchair. Her husband can always be found at her side, comforting her, looking for things he can do for her, seeking ways to be of service. These people have a lovely marriage—because the husband is an unselfish hero.

On the other hand, a young man of twenty-two had been brought up by his parents to expect everything in life without working for it much, if at all. Rang the wedding bells, and the need to support his wife began to beat down on him. Listening to him, you would have thought that he was one of the world's great martyrs because he had to get up at eight o'clock every morning to work. When his wife announced that she was going to have a baby, he went into deep thought and concluded that she probably would expect him to extend little courtesies in view of her condition—courtesies like helping her carry heavy boxes from the grocery store. When last seen, he had deserted his wife and had lit out for a distant shore, where he can spend all his time thinking only of himself and his selfish interests.

Of course, people change during their lives. The characteristics someone displays at eighteen might not be quite the same as those he or she will have at thirty-eight. But people usually don't change as drastically as you might think. A thoroughly selfish person of eighteen might become somewhat less selfish with the years. But it is unlikely that he will ever be truly unselfish.

Some young people indulge in wishful thinking when this subject comes up. They think that, somehow, after marriage, everything will be different. In their dream world, the person who now always seems to be seeking an argument will become meek and docile. The egomaniac will become a shining example of modesty. The person who can't spend a quiet evening at home will suddenly curl up, night after night, with good books.

But let me warn you that those "miracles" are so rare that for all practical purposes you can forget about them. The person you marry is going to have the same character traits as the person you knew before marriage. In fact, he or she is likely to have them to an even greater extent, for our fundamental characteristics tend to become stronger with age, rather than weaker.

For that reason, one of the soundest pieces of advice given to young men and women in sizing up a prospective mate is to—

Look Ahead Ten Years!

Ten years from now you will be sitting across the supper table from a slightly paunchy man or a somewhat weary woman. And if God is good to you, three or four little demons of varying ages (and varying lung capacities) will be sitting between you and your spouse, each clamoring for more food, all of them making conversation between Pop and Mom well-nigh impossible.

Later on in the evening, when your pride-and-joys are safely tucked in bed (following a few bedroom riots), John will likely be comfortably settled in some easy chair, sipping a can of beer and watching the contemporary "Untouchables," while Mary continues to drag herself around the house picking up the day's debris.

Finally, the two of you are alone. And you talk. You may even argue, one complaining about the lack of money, the other about the housekeeping. It is surprising how easily tired people can express themselves forcefully over doctor's bills, nights out, in-laws, even beer-drinking. Shortly, either or both of you will shuffle off to bed with a simple "good night," hoping for the rest that will enable you to rise the next day, to begin a round of duties very much like those of the day just finished.

This is hardly the nightly meeting of Prince Charming and his Cinderella, the unending drama played so many times in the reveries of the young. And yet, this generally is the married life all of you will experience.

Unglamorous, you say. Well, it all depends on what you mean by glamor. To the very young person, marriage, I suppose, means moonlight and roses, just as for the junior seminarian, the priesthood means the majestic figure in the pulpit. *And going through the romantic stage of life is a valuable experience—as long as you are aware of the reality ahead.*

Marriage, like the priesthood, means work, responsibility, self-sacrifice. In one way, it is easier than the priesthood because you have help. In another way, it is harder, because working intimately with a member of the opposite sex during the "worse," "poorer" and "sickness" periods is not at all easy.

What you really must do during courtship is to look beyond the romance (beyond the first years of marriage) and try to picture what the other party will be like ten years later. In ten years you will be grateful for two things: 1. A husband (or wife) who is responsible and easy to get along with; 2. A husband (or wife) who likes children and is happy in creating a child, not only at the moment of conception, but day in and day out.

I have known many "romantic" marriages to break up—and very early, too. I have never met a good, congenial couple, getting along together and satisfied with the simple works of marriage, who broke up because one or the other wasn't glamorous enough. The football hero may give you a moment of ecstasy. The math student may give you a lifetime of contentment and accomplishment.

Which brings us back to the word *glamor*. The thirty-year-old man or woman defines it differently than you do. Ten years from now, you'll have a different definition, too. Sitting in the midst of that bedlam at the supper table, many Johns look across at their Marys quite gratified that they're such wonderful mothers. And the Marys, by the time they are thirty, find a certain restfulness and security in good, weekly paychecks and husbands who can be talked to, even argued with.

After married people really settle down, who wants a steady diet of excitement? Love at that stage is a little quieter, a little purer. Just being together in silence then means much more than those earlier long nights spent chatting at the soda fountain.

Giving up the summer vacation in order that money is available for Junior's tuition, sitting up all night with a sick child in crisis and finding him alive and well the following morning, making a decision together about a recently widowed mother or father; these are the satisfactions that make marriage worthwhile for mature Christians. And this is the real love that the Hollywood script writers (who often have loved so little) find hard to define.

The point is: We want you to enter marriage with the *emo-*

tion of youth; but we want you to have the *reasonableness of maturity,* too. There is every hope that you will be in love when you marry; there is no reason why you should be silly fools.

And you should be thinking straight now, while your mind is uncluttered by the sometime mirages of romance.

A young man came to see me the other day—the product of a good family and the graduate of a Catholic college. He is going to marry a disreputable woman of three months' acquaintance. He would not see how wrong this is. He would not *let* himself see.

We can only suggest that you never put yourself in the position of making an important decision to marry, blinded by emotion.

Four years ago, I stood a few feet behind my mother as she prayed for a final moment over the corpse of my father, just before they closed the coffin. Without realizing I was in earshot, she whispered: "Good-bye, Charlie. It's been a good life. I will see you in heaven."

This is the ending to which you should aspire, for in the last analysis, it is the *ending,* not the beginning, that counts.

14. LET'S TALK ABOUT MARRIAGE

If you can accept one simple fact of life, you will be able to understand what you must know in order to date successfully and to build a happy marriage. This fact is that God never acts without good reasons.

When you realize this, you'll be able to consider why He made two sexes. As we know from the Old Testament, He didn't have to do this. If He wanted to, He could have arranged matters so that there were only men to do the work of the world. But He first created Adam, and then—"because it is not good for man to be alone"—he created Eve.

In deciding upon two sexes, God also decided that each sex should have a specific job to do. He gave to the male one basic physical and emotional setup, and He gave to the female a different one. Where He made the male strong, He made the female relatively weak. Where He made the female strong, the male was relatively weak. By combining their resources, they could accomplish what neither could achieve alone.

After God created Adam and Eve, He told them: "Increase and multiply." Thus He gave them a plain order to procreate, and to care for their young until the children were able to care for themselves. By His will, therefore, Adam and Eve became the first husband and wife, the first father and mother.

From all of this, we know that God created the institution of marriage. And we also know that Jesus Christ, His Son, had definite ideas about marriage. For instance, Jesus said that "What God hath joined together, let no man put asunder." Thus he taught us that marriage as far as God is concerned, is to be a lifetime union.

Since marriage is God's invention, He alone has the right to set up the rules of the game. And if we want to use the institution He created, we will have to play His game according to His requirements.

This is the Catholic position. It's also the traditional viewpoint that has been held by the churches—all churches, in fact —up until the present time. But now some people are denying that God is the author of marriage. They claim it is man's invention—and therefore that we can play the game according to our own rules. We can do what we want: Divorce at will, have children as our whim dictates, be unfaithful to our mate if we feel like it, be completely free to do whatever suits us at the moment. They deny, in effect, that God has any right to tell us what to do.

Suppose you walked into a strange home and saw a father lounging in the kitchen while his three-year-old son toyed with matches. You'd say that the father had every right to tell his child not to play with matches because they were too dangerous. If the boy wouldn't listen, you'd certainly say the father should take the matches away: Since he has the boy's interests at heart, you'd say he has the right to prevent him from hurting himself.

Just as a father must set his child on the proper path to help him achieve happiness, God to an even greater extent must set up rules so that we can achieve happiness not only here on earth but also in the world to come. A child who won't follow his father's rules, will find himself unhappy. And so too will unhappiness be inevitable for anyone who won't follow the rules God has established.

The little child might think his father was a killjoy by taking away the matches. Sometimes we also might find God's rules difficult to follow. With our limited knowledge—much more limited compared to God's than the knowledge of a child compared to his father's—we might think God won't let us be happy. But to get back to the point I made earlier, He does everything for a reason. And when He set up His rules for marriage, He did so to help you achieve happiness—even if you don't realize it at the moment.

God is interested in you personally. When He calls some of you to the vocation of marriage, He wants you to have the blessings of children—the satisfaction of rearing them when they're young and the comfort they can give you when you're old. Because He knows that love is one of the greatest gifts in life, he wants you to love both your partner and your children to the greatest possible extent. But this is possible *only* in a marriage that is set up along the lines he established—a marriage for life, where one partner must always be faithful to the other, where husband and wife cheerfully do their job of bringing up their children.

Let me sum up what Catholic marriage is:

1. It is a creation of Almighty God—an institution He made for a specific purpose.

2. In accordance with the order He gave Adam and Eve to "increase and multiply," marriage is primarily for the procreation and education of children. But God had other reasons too. He created it as a means by which a man and woman could complement each other's personality and find comfort and solace in each other's company. And He also created it so that a man and woman could express their physical love for each other in a legitimate way.

In the following pages I'll try to describe God's purposes more fully, and point out the greatest danger young people face today—the danger that they'll forget all about the One Who created marriage and established the rules. This is of prime importance, because the false idea that marriage is a game that man can play any way he wants is what you'll have to guard against constantly from the time of your first date.

"Modern" Marriage Vs. Catholic Marriage

Suppose someone tried to hand you this advice:

"The whole idea of marriage is to get as much out of it as you can. Don't be a sucker and marry for any other reason.

"Try to avoid having children. They tie you down too much.

"Remember that you can end your marriage easily, so don't stand for any nonsense from your partner. If you ever decide that you haven't made the best possible choice, or if the obligations of your marriage begin to hurt, get a divorce. Or if someone comes along who looks good to you, get rid of your first partner just as you'd dispose of an old car.

"Your marriage is like a suit of clothes or a dress. You should be able to step out of it any time you want."

You'd certainly know that you were receiving the worst possible advice—that anybody who believes marriage is a grab bag for the selfish is as far off the beam as you can get.

You might say that a person who gave such advice would be like the medical student who wanted to be a doctor. But he decided that he'd never help a dying patient if it interfered with a TV program he wanted to see.

Suppose a young man, studying at the seminary decided that after he became a priest, he'd never say a Mass if it forced him to get up earlier than 11:00 A.M. Or suppose a girl training to be a nurse resolved that she'd quit any job where she'd face the sight of blood.

I know a lad who was thinking about the career he'd like to follow in life. He had been left a bit of money by his father, and he thought he'd like to open a store where he could be his own boss. Since he enjoyed sports of all kinds, he thought he'd like to get into the sporting goods business. Fine—except for one thing. All through elementary and high school, his worst subject had always been Math. In fact, he hated to have to add even two numbers. Whenever he bought something at a store, he relied on the shopkeeper's honesty to give him the right change.

A friend told this lad that any businessman has to spend a great deal of time doing arithmetic. Otherwise, how can he be sure that he's getting enough money for the stuff he sells? How can he know whether he's charging enough to cover the cost of his goods, the rent, light, heat and all the other expenses of running the store, as well as his own profit? "Oh, well," the would-be merchant answered, "I can always hire somebody to do my arithmetic."

The friend laughed. "And who are you going to hire," he asked, "to make sure that the man won't cheat you?"

You'd say, of course, that people like this who are unwilling to do *everything* the job calls for would be better off if they stopped training immediately and took up something else. Because they're obviously unwilling to prepare themselves. You'd argue—correctly—that anyone who wanted to be a priest, a nurse, a doctor, a businessman or to follow any other profession would have to fulfill all the duties involved in those vocations.

Could You Dictate to an Employer?

No man would hire you if you asked for a job and then presented him with a list of all the things involved in the job that you wouldn't do. He'd laugh at you—or throw you out of his office.

As you continue to date and begin to think more seriously about your future, you may be shocked at the number of persons who will do everything expected of them in any other job, but who balk at doing the work God requires of them in marriage. In fact, so many "moderns" operate this way that your Christian ideas about marriage may often prove very unpopular.

You'll discover, however, that such "moderns" usually have no clear idea of what marriage should be. True, they put up a brave front of knowing what it's all about. But you'll often find that when a crisis arises in their lives, they're bewildered, confused, and miserable—all because they haven't abided by the rules set down by the Creator.

For now, however, they seem to have one fixed idea. "Do it our way," they argue. "It's easier."

It certainly seems so—at least for a time. Suppose that after a few years of marriage, a wife contracts a disease that leaves her bedridden. What's easier for the husband than to put on his hat and coat, leave home and head for a place where a quick divorce on trumped-up charges can relieve him of his responsibility to care for her?

Or suppose that a wife, married a few years, now finds that a rich man is interested in her and can give her luxuries her husband can't afford. What's easier than to walk out and leave her husband to cope with the motherless children she leaves behind?

The Problems of Married People

Let me say that every marriage I have ever observed has had some difficulties. Just as there has never been a body of water without a ripple or a wave, so too there has never been a marriage without some ups and downs. A permanently calm body of water is impossible as long as the wind can blow. So too is it impossible to have a perfectly tranquil marriage between two individuals with different personalities and backgrounds.

What are some of the typical danger areas of marriage? Based on the experiences of many marriage counselors along with my own, I would list the major potential sore spots as follows:

In-laws. Several studies have shown that the biggest problem of some newlyweds is adjusting to what they might consider "interference" by their relatives. Your husband's mother may seem to be trying to tell you how to run your home. Your wife's father may seem to be setting down rules for you in your job. Your brother-in-law may get too personal in his wisecracks. Your sister-in-law and her boy friend may turn up at your home for a free meal whenever they want. And so on.

Of course, you marry the man or woman. But if you find his or her in-laws too hard to take, if you think they may be too bossy or that your prospective mate might be too easily influenced by their opinions, you can expect to have some rough moments. If the trouble were greater than you could handle, your marriage itself would be in danger.

In-laws can help your marriage, too. One man without living parents married a girl whose parents also were dead. This couple had difficult financial problems in their early years together, and had no in-laws to provide them with help. Both probably often wished they had a father-in-law or mother-in-law to turn to.

New Responsibilities. A young man marries and suddenly has a family to support. No longer can he go or come freely, spending as he wishes, thinking of his own pleasures first. The young woman becomes a mother and suddenly faces the obligations of caring for her child. How will the husband or wife accept these new responsibilities? If they fail to rise to them, and fail to do all that is expected of them—there's bound to be trouble.

Money matters. Serious money problems in marriage usually are the symptoms of other difficulties. But a man or woman who's at one extreme or the other—who's either too cheap or too much of a spendthrift—may be extremely hard to live with. A husband and wife ought to have the same general ideas about money, otherwise, they'll probably have difficulty.

One couple have a free and easy attitude about their income. They can get into debt up to their necks without being bothered in the least. Another couple consider it a disgrace if they owe a cent. Both couples are happily married, because in each case the husband and wife agree on this matter. Sparks would fly, however, if the first man had married the second woman. Then they would have had entirely different ideas about a tool they use every day of their lives.

Bad habits like excessive drinking or gambling. A study of fifteen hundred divorce cases revealed the startling fact that excessive drinking was cited as a cause of the breakup more often than cruelty, adultery, bigamy, fraud and sexual complaints combined. This does not mean that a person who enjoys wine or beer with meals or an occasional drink is doomed. But someone who always thinks he needs a drink to have a good time is starting out in the worst possible way.

Gambling can also grow into a raging disease. Here again it's okay in moderation. A dollar bet on the outcome of a ball game or a horse race may be a harmless diversion. But some men regularly lose their paychecks at the race track, while their children are at home hungry and without shoes.

Discussion of disagreements. A husband and wife will often find it necessary to settle their different attitudes on various problems they encounter. If they can't discuss these things in an understanding way, they will find that even slight differences of opinion can turn into full-fledged battles. It is important to have a partner you can talk to freely—not a tyrant who thinks his or her word is law.

How you disagree over minor matters now may supply a good preview of how your problems will be solved later. First, of course, brace yourself for the inevitable: On many questions, every husband and wife hold different opinions. They are bound to have opposing ideas about how the household should be run, where to spend their vacation, what to do with their income, and so on. Unless they can resolve such differences in a calm, loving manner, they may find themselves growing further apart.

A few years ago, newspapers carried the story of a husband and wife who got a divorce because they couldn't agree on whether to sleep with the windows open or shut. Of course, it was a stupid cause for breaking up a marriage, but you can be sure that if they couldn't agree on a simple matter like that, they couldn't agree on hundreds of other similar matters that crop up in the course of every marriage.

Lifetime ambitions. As in the case of money matters, the

couples who agree on the objectives they hope to achieve in life are likely to make the best adjustments. But potential danger exists if, for instance, the husband wants to improve his lot in life dramatically while his wife is content to live as she always has done.

Sometimes a man is happy in his work but will never get to be a boss. His overly ambitious wife may nag him to get a better job until the marriage itself is wrecked. Please note this: I don't say that a lot of ambition is desirable or that no ambition is desirable. I do say that unless a couple agree about it and have roughly the same amount of ambition, they may find it becoming a sore spot in their marriage.

Of course, the major questions of life are "Why are you here?" and "Where are you going?" The goal for all Christians is to save their souls. If you have salvation-ambition as the crowning goal of life, you will certainly want to marry someone who shares this objective with you. Ditto for all the things that will help you reach your goal: The practice of your religion, the way you educate your children, and so on.

Marriage is like a special automobile that required two people to drive it. It would be impossible to go any place with such a car if one person was giving it the gas and stepping on the clutch while the other had his foot firmly pressed against the brakes. But that's how it is in a marriage in which the husband and wife don't agree on fundamentals.

Christ Asks for Heroes

People who think they'll flee when times get tough or a more alluring opportunity presents itself, are living in a fool's paradise. Life doesn't work that way. It reminds us of the time Our Lord was fasting on the mountain and the devil appeared and offered the world if Jesus would worship him. Our Lord felt the temptations that such promises afford to human weaknesses, but He also knew how the so-called "easy" life can lead to ruination. In turning down the devil He performed an act of heroism.

God also expects you to be a hero. Better than you, He knows that the flesh is weak, and He takes it into consideration in judging mankind. But he doesn't say, "Because you're weak, you don't have to obey the rules." Rather he says this: "Obey my rules. But if you are so weak that you are honestly unable to reach the standards I have set, I will forgive you."

In a nutshell, that's the difference between modern ideas about marriage and the Christian idea of marriage. The modern idea is that man is weak and that the rules should therefore be soft and easy. The Christian ideal says that we should make our flesh work for our spirit, and not let the spirit be dominated by the flesh. The hero in battle overcomes his natural tendency to be afraid and climbs out of his foxhole to accept the enemy's challenge. He doesn't take "the easy way out" and cringe in a corner of his dugout.

It may well be that you'll have to be a Christian hero. In holding fast to your beliefs and trying to live up to your ideals of what marriage should be, you may find yourself with a viewpoint opposite that of most of the people around you. Your belief—that marriage was made by God, is intended for two persons unto death, and has as its main purpose the procreation and education of children—all these are unpopular in some quarters.

Resolve now to be a hero—to do what's right regardless of what others may think. God expects such heroism of you, just as your country expects a soldier to fight for its defense in time of war. And just as your country honors its heroes, so too will you merit your reward according to how well you have lived up to the standards God has set.

15. THE BIRTH CONTROL MENTALITY

This is the tale of two ladies who lived in the same town. One lived in a big house at the top of the hill. She had servants to do everything she wanted—draw her morning bath, bring breakfast on a tray to her bedside, open her morning mail, drive her to shops where she could buy expensive gowns from Paris.

Needless to say, she was rich. She now had money because she and her husband, early in their marriage, had decided that they did not want to have the "trouble" of children. They were so busy making money that they could not give a child the love and attention that they would have to give. And so they practiced birth control. Now in her late years, this woman has "everything." Yet she actually lives a miserable life, because she does not have the most precious gift of all—the love of children near and dear to her.

At the other end of town is a woman who gets up early in the morning, makes breakfast for her six children, sees that the younger ones are dressed properly, and pushes them off to school. She is busy all day long, doing things for her family. The high spot of her day occurs when her youngsters return one by one with outspread arms, to greet her with true affection.

This woman has no easy time financially. Unlike the woman at the top of the hill, she cannot afford regular visits to the beauty parlor or the expensive dress shop. But when she completes her day, she can rest herself hand in hand with her husband, feeling amply repaid for her labors of love with the respect that her family bestows upon her.

Which of these women is truly the richer? The first has the things of the world, but she has permitted herself to dry up spiritually because of her selfish unwillingness to share herself with other human beings. The second woman's credit rating at the local department stores is not nearly so high, but her blessed children are more precious to her than any diamond that has ever been mined.

I have known many elderly men and women who have had an opportunity to look back upon their lifetimes. Some were highly successful in the world—executives, professional men, owners of prospering businesses. Some were employees who worked for wages all their lives and seldom had more than a few hundred dollars in the bank at any time. Yet I have rarely met a man or woman who, looking back, felt they had too many children. Parents of two or three youngsters, for example, wish they had four or five at least. One woman with fifteen children said that one of the saddest moments in her life came when her last child began to walk and she realized that she soon would no longer be able to hold a baby of her own in her arms.

Of course, this is not the viewpoint you will get from many people around you. The story you may get from outside the Faith is that children are a burden. That they cost too much. That they take up too much of your time. That it's smart to limit yourself to none, one or two. That it's wrong to have more than you can send to an Ivy League college.

This is the "birth control mentality." Let's consider for a minute how wrong it is. We believe, of course, that God is the Creator of us all. He has given you your reproductive powers for the primary purpose of propagating the human race. And therefore any use of those powers which ignores God's purpose in giving them to you is wrong.

The First Task of Marriage

When you marry, you must agree to live in marriage in the way God had in mind when he created the sacrament. That's understandable. If you wanted to play a game of tennis, for instance, it would be reasonable to expect you to play the game according to the rules. That's why they were created. And the first rule of marriage is that it be used for the procreating and educating of children. God made that perfectly plain when His first words to Adam and Eve were, "Increase and multiply." When two people marry, therefore, they should be willing to bring children into the world and to give them the best possible training and example so that they may be able to save their souls and live with God for an eternity in heaven.

Parenthood is and always has been regarded with awe by the races of mankind. In fact, if you stop to think about it, you'll realize that it's an almost miraculous power which God gives to a mother and father—an almost unbelievable opportunity to create a being that can be taught to know God and to serve Him for an eternity. A mother and father are creating a work of art that the greatest of painters, sculptors and others could never duplicate. Even if all of them got together on a single work, it wouldn't be nearly so beautiful or impressive as the little child that God gives husbands and wives the opportunity to create in marriage.

The desire for children is instilled in mankind. Through the ages, man in his native wisdom has always regarded parents as among the most blessed of creatures. A baby has always been considered as "a gift from heaven."

Little Children Are a Joy

In our society, there are many people who seem to be peddling the idea that having children is a burden. Nonsense! An obligation to God? Yes. A responsibility? Yes. But the little child brings more happiness into the home than any sacrifice the parents may experience in having him.

Speak to a mother—even at the end of a hard day—about this. She may be tired and may do a great deal of work in caring for her children. But ask her if she would part with them for a more comfortable life—a bigger house maybe, or a better car, or a vacation at a swanky seaside resort.

The answer you get would run something like this: "Not in the world would I give up my children!" In fact, if a woman said she'd exchange her children for the passing, material pleasures of life, you'd probably think there was something wrong with her.

This does not mean that the Church requires husbands and wives to have an unlimited number of children in an endless procession. Pope Pius XI listed four conditions that might excuse husbands and wives from the obligations of parenthood. These conditions might be medical, economic, social or eugenical. Let's say a wife has a serious illness and her doctor says her condition would worsen if she had a baby. Or suppose the chances are that her husband will not live long enough to be a father to the child. There's no obligation in cases like these to bring an infant into the world.

An economic reason: Suppose the family is having a hard time as it is, and a baby would throw the budget out of whack.

A social condition: A soldier has been told that he'll be shipped out of the country or far away from his home town for several years. Or suppose a man and his family are stuck in a one-room flat and couldn't find space for another child. (This happened to quite a few people after the war.)

Eugenical: Let's say that there has been a record of serious illness in the family (like a certain mental illness) that is likely to be transmitted to a child.

If any of these conditions exist, if both the husband and wife agree about what to do, and if they would not be in danger of committing other sins, they may make use of the "Rhythm Method." Let me explain briefly: There are only a few days in a woman's regular monthly cycle when she is fertile—capable of conceiving a child. If a husband and wife do not have physical relations at this time, they will not become parents. (It is always wrong to use artificial methods to prevent birth, because such methods directly interfere with nature.)

As you can see, the Church's attitude about parenthood is fair and reasonable. She does not demand more than any Catholic with the right dispositions can fulfill. Those who find fault with our position are usually those who argue that it is okay to avoid having children for any reason you can think of, and that it is perfectly all right to use artificial means to defeat the very purpose which God intended when He created the reproductive organs.

The happiest and most satisfied people in life are those who are not afraid to think big—to carry burdens which weaker people would be afraid of, to accept challenges the less daring would shrink from, and to be generous in their attitudes toward God and their fellowmen.

It takes a big heart to undertake the responsibility of a large family. But the human rewards, as well as those from God Himself, will make you forever glad that you were courageous enough to do the great work He asked of you.

16. WHY MARRIAGE IS FOR LIFE

Alicia had perhaps the worst memory of anybody I ever met. If her mother sent her to the store for three items, Alicia would probably forget one of them before she took ten steps from her house. When she was given a homework assignment, she'd forget it while searching for a pencil to write it down in her notebook. If she made a date to meet friends at a certain time and place, they could never be sure she would be there at the appointed hour. Her mind was like a sieve.

For some reason, however, she knew one sentence cold. She could recite it frontward, backward, or starting in the middle and working toward either end. The sentence was the solemn vow a man and woman take at the altar rail:

"I take thee for my lawful wife (husband) to have and to hold from this day forward, for better, for worse, for richer, for poorer, in sickness and in health, until death do us part."

Psychologists say we remember those things we want to remember. And it is obvious that Alicia knew where her best interests lay. After graduating from high school, she took a job as a secretary and within three years she married the boss's nephew.

You yourself could do worse than to memorize the marriage vow and to think about its meaning. It means that you agree to remain as husband and wife in spite of any catastrophes, calamities, misfortunes, mishaps, exasperations, griefs, illnesses, bitterness, gloom, heartache, miseries, nuisances, vexations, bother or pother that may later come up. Moreover, it means that you will keep this pledge until either of you dies.

What Our Lord Taught Us

In the world we live in, there are many pressures trying to make Catholics forget that marriage was designed by God to last for life. Our Lord Himself taught that matrimony must be permanent when He said: "What therefore God has joined together, let no man put asunder." These simple words mean that the marriage bond cannot be broken by any man.

That divorce is illegal has always been taught by the Church down through the ages. For example, St. Paul said: "A woman is bound as long as her husband is alive, but if her husband dies, she is free. Let her marry whom she pleases, only let it be in the Lord." As recently as 1946, Pope Pius XII formally stated that a valid marriage can be "dissolved by no human power and by no other causes but death."

Christian countries have always looked upon divorce with horror. It has only been recently that some persons have decided that marriage can be broken at will. As a result, you can find in the newspapers a wide variety of ridiculous reasons why men and women are allowed to end their relationship. One man submitted a photo of rings around the bathtub to prove that his wife was a poor housekeeper and therefore an unworthy mate. A woman claimed that her husband refused to eat breakfast at home, and therefore caused her extreme "mental anguish."

Divorce often creates more problems than it solves. In fact, those in a position to know say that most divorced couples would gladly go back to their married way of life if they could only swallow their pride. For a divorced man or woman in our society often leads a terrifyingly lonely life.

Moreover, divorce always represents defeat—a terrible personal tragedy. When a couple who married in the Church agree to a divorce, it means that they have failed in an agreement with Christ. You would be shocked if a priest decided to chuck the priesthood and go into some other occupation. You'd think it was sacrilegious, because he was walking out on the job he vowed to perform for the rest of his life. Couples who rush to the divorce courts also fail in the job they have promised to do for God.

The children of a broken marriage often suffer even more than the man and woman involved. Often, the children must choose between two parents they love. They have feelings of guilt when they display affection for one parent in the other's presence. During the bitter wrangling that divorce often involves, the child is forced to conclude that one of his parents, at least, is unworthy—a terrible thought for a child to have.

On the other hand, when you accept the law of God prohibiting divorce, you are helped to make a better marriage to begin with. You are required to consider prayerfully whether marriage is indeed the state in life God wishes for you, and also whether your intended would make a suitable partner. When you know that you must live with this decision for a lifetime, you will be prepared to work and pray to make a right and proper choice.

And when you marry, you and your partner are both willing to make concessions. You have to try to get along, because you have no other choice. So you work to settle your differences and achieve a satisfactory relationship.

The Bonds of a Catholic Marriage

In fact, one of the little-recognized bonuses of a Catholic marriage is that a sincere man and woman must be willing to make any sacrifices to keep their union in a good, healthy condition. With that attitude, they are more willing to look for peaceful compromises if any problems arise.

A non-Catholic woman was talking to a Catholic friend, emphasizing how valuable this little clause in the marriage contract was worth.

"When I married," this woman said, "I had the idea that I'd get a divorce if my husband didn't act exactly the way that I wanted him to. So whenever we had an argument, I kept wondering whether I ought to pack my clothes and fly to Reno. I kept telling him that if he didn't like the way things were going we could just call it quits. One day he took me at my word.

"Almost before I knew it, I was divorced and he was married to another woman. I know now that getting a divorce was the biggest mistake I ever made, and I don't think I would have made it if I had been determined at the beginning of my marriage that I would do everything possible to make a success of it."

Divorce court judges, marriage counselors and other experts all agree that most couples can get along together if they really want to—if they would only try to patch up their troubles and to understand the other person's point of view. In fact, where laws require couples to "cool off" and try to solve their marriage problems before getting a divorce, a surprisingly large number discover they can make a go of it.

How can you avoid divorce in your life? You should hold an idea of marriage in your mind which is vastly different from the "easy-come, easy-go" attitude prevalent outside the Church. Think of the Christian home as a "little church"—as a place God Himself developed to enable men and women to save their souls, and also as a means of creating and educating children to know, love and serve Him.

Think of your home as an extension of God's Kingdom on earth—as a sanctuary where husband, wife and children all can achieve their destiny as children of God. Regard marriage as an institution which is worth preserving at all costs. Enter it determined to do whatever is necessary to make it a blessed place in the sight of God. Do this and divorce—and all the failure that it involves—will never plague your sacred union.

The Impediments to Marriage

Whenever someone gets a gray hair in his head, he seems to feel qualified to review the past, compare it with the present, and make a short speech about the "good old days." I probably have done my share of that, but I must admit that there are occasions when modern times have quite an advantage over days gone by.

This becomes particularly apparent when you read about the shennanigans in medieval times, for example, among people about to get married. Books are full of tales of men who stabbed others in dark alleys in order to marry their widows, of men who kidnapped unwilling brides, of men and women who were mugged or drugged and then dragged to the altar. Down through the years, all kinds of devious schemes have been attempted to defeat the basic idea of marriage, which is the voluntary contract between a man and woman to live as husband and wife for the rest of their days.

Of course, the Church has resisted efforts made by men and women in every age to get around this fundamental purpose. That's why she has set up specific rules telling you what type of person you may not marry, and under what conditions your marriage would not be valid. Unlike the so-called "good old days," however, persons now seldom use cloak-and-dagger tactics to marry in defiance of the laws of the Church.

When the Church cites what are known as "impediments" to a valid marriage, she means that you cannot truly marry before a priest if such impediments exist. Space is too limited to list and explain all of the impediments, but some of the more common ones are these:

Persons with a close blood relationship cannot marry. For instance, a brother cannot marry his sister, nor can first or second cousins marry unless a special dispensation is granted. Similarly, a godparent may not marry his godchild, nor may a baptized person marry the person who performed the Baptism.

Anyone who has been ordained a priest or has made a solemn profession of vows in a religious order cannot validly marry. Nor can a person who is permanently incapable of performing the marital act. Such a person is said to be impotent.

No one can be validly married unless he understands the nature of marriage and freely consents to the contract. Thus someone who was drunk, insane or drugged at the time of the ceremony is not validly married, nor is anyone who was forced to marry by threats against his life. A person under twenty-one must submit his or her parents' written consent before being permitted to marry in the Church.

Another impediment is "wrong consent." For example, a man might go through the ceremony, all the while planning not to live up to the rules of married life. He might think that he would get a divorce if anything went wrong, or would never permit his wife to have a child. He would not be giving proper consent to marriage, because he was not willing to abide by all conditions of it.

There Are No "Easy" Annulments

An impediment that occurs frequently now is the one by which someone already married cannot remarry unless the first marriage has been annulled, or the first partner has died. This is an important point to remember in these times when divorce is so prevalent—so important, in fact, that I would advise any young person to avoid dating, going steady with, or becoming engaged to, any person who has been married unless it is clear beyond doubt that he or she is now free to marry in the Church.

One girl met a man eight years older than herself and began seeing him regularly. If it ever occurred to her to wonder why a man as old, handsome and charming as he was had never married before, she refused to give it a second thought.

Finally, after she had been seeing him for months, he admitted that he was married, but said that he had applied for an annulment on the grounds that his wife had been insane. The girl took him at his word and continued to see him regularly, expecting the annulment at almost any moment. After several years, the annulment was denied. But by then the couple had become too involved with each other to break off their relationship. They have been living in sin ever since.

The girl in this case was basically a nice girl when she met this man. But one thing led to another until she was trapped into the ugly life she now leads. Her first big mistake was to begin dating someone who had been married before and who did not now have an "all-clear" signal to marry again.

In every crowd, there's always a Philadelphia lawyer. When the subject of impediments comes up, he raises his hand with a question:

"Can't a Catholic couple marry and then, if things don't work out as they plan, can't they claim there was an impediment and their marriage was not valid at all?"

In this way, the legal beagles reason, the couple could get an annulment, then marry again in the Church. The flaw in this reasoning is that the Church does not hand out annulments like trading stamps. A man and woman who marry before a priest are presumed to be free to marry and to fulfill all the requirements for marriage. If they later claim that one of these essential requirements was lacking, they have to prove, beyond doubt, that the marriage was not valid. Such a thing is extremely difficult to do. It takes years in many cases and also involves a great deal of expense.

Believe me, it's not worth it. Anyone who marries with his eye on a loophole is not marrying with the proper attitude. He should stay away from marriage until he is ready, willing and able to make a valid contract for life.

Before You Become Engaged

Two of the shortest words in the language are "I," and "do." But put them together and they make the longest sentence in the world—a sentence for life.

Certainly no other two words you ever utter will have as much meaning as these two. For when you utter them, you promise to fulfill all the sacred responsibilities that fall upon a Christian husband or wife. Quite a lot of promises to make with two syllables!

You'd better thoroughly understand what these words mean because, as I have emphasized and as your teachers in religion have told you and will continue to tell you, once you say them you will have to live with them for life.

Before you utter them, you should be sure that you have the right intentions about the purposes of marriage. You should be able to answer the following questions which touch on the very nature of the marriage relationship.

Do you understand that marriage cannot be dissolved in any way, except by death? The average American, with only newspapers to go by, might think that divorce is a way of life in itself—that all you have to do is get a divorce whenever a little trouble arises in the marriage. As a Catholic, you know, of course, that marriage is permanent—that, as Christ said, "What God hath joined together, let no man put asunder."

Do you intend to be faithful to your husband or wife at all times? When you say "I do," you pledge yourself to your partner. You promise that neither by thought nor act will you engage in intimate relationship with any member of the opposite sex. In this time of loose morality, it may seem old-fashioned to insist that husband and wife always must be true to each other and must practice chastity in their relationship.

But the law of God has been in force since the beginning of time, and will continue in force until the end of time.

Do you understand that the primary purpose of marriage is the propagation and education of children? Of course, God in His wisdom may have not provided you or your mate with the necessary physical powers to become a parent. You, of course, are not responsible if you cannot have children. The important thing is that if God so wants it, you are willing to be a parent, to bring into the world little souls you will strive to educate so that they may one day reach the Kingdom of Heaven.

Do you realize that artificial birth control is a sin? You would not be entering marriage with the proper frame of mind if you proposed to use contraceptives or other products designed to prevent birth. The Rhythm Method—which is based on the natural, God-given period in each month when a woman cannot conceive a child—is proper when used in accordance with the principles laid down by the Popes.

Do you intend to allow your intended mate the full measure of his or her rights to participate in the marital act? There must be no intention to have the kind of marriage sometimes seen on the screen—one in which a couple are husband and wife in name only.

If you can read between the lines of the questions above, you will discover something that all have in common. It is that you are required to believe things which most non-Catholics obviously do not now believe. You are asked to stand up and to identify yourself as a member of a minority group— the group that believes that Marriage is a sacrament instituted by God. That it is for life. That it has as its primary purpose the propagation and education of children. That it must be between two persons who pledge themselves, completely and without qualification, to each other.

You have been exposed to a different philosophy of life, the wreckage of which is evident all around us. This is the philosophy that says a couple can pursue their own selfish in-

terests, forget their obligations to use their powers of reproduction as God intended, and get rid of each other as they
might dispose of an old dress or a worn suit.

As a Catholic, you will have to strengthen your own beliefs
so that you can uphold them against the opposition of the
majority all around you. You will have to struggle to make a
good marriage that can survive all the temptations of married
life. But in strengthening your marriage, you will strengthen
yourself. And in making your marriage a more blessed thing
in the eyes of God, you will be making yourself—and your
partner—more blessed in His sight as well.

What You Should Know about the Sacrament

Let's say you have done everything you should in thinking
about your prospects for making a good marriage with this
guy or gal you have in mind and you're ready to take the
Big Plunge. You should become familiar with the great sacrament of Matrimony that you will receive when you seal your
marriage contract before the priest.

In thinking about this, imagine for a moment that a king,
president, or a prime minister accepted an invitation to have
dinner at your house. Suppose you had weeks to prepare for
his coming, but you were the type of person who put everything off until the last minute. Suppose that on the day of the
dinner, you slept late, left the dirty dishes in the sink, allowed
your living and dining rooms to remain messed up, and spent
your time chatting with friends. Suppose that half an hour
before dinner time, you went to the refrigerator to see what
leftovers you could scrape together for the evening meal. And
suppose that you greeted your guest in old clothes, with dirty
hands and uncombed hair, and with a cigarette dangling from
your lips.

Wouldn't people be justified in saying that you were out
of your mind—that you didn't deserve such a guest of honor,

and that he couldn't be blamed if he took to his heels and walked right out of your house because of the lack of respect you had shown?

Of course, they would be right. Because it is the custom for people to extend themselves for any guests—but especially to show deference and consideration to those who hold honored positions in the country. In fact, if a head of state were to visit you, you probably would be beside yourself with excitement for weeks in advance, making sure that your house was scrubbed from top to bottom, and that the dinner would be of the finest food you could buy, prepared in the best way imaginable. Truly, you would try to make the meal fit for a king.

When you marry in the Church, you invite the King of Kings to your wedding. Indeed, you solemnly pledge yourself before Him for life, and you are assured of His continuing help to enable you to fulfill the role you are undertaking.

Because you marry in the presence of God, the marriage ceremony itself is a sacred, holy rite—one of the most significant religious rites of your life. So, you should be prepared to marry in the holiest way possible. You should prepare yourself to be worthy in the presence of Jesus, to a much greater extent than you would prepare yourself to enter the presence of an earthly monarch.

Because holy things should not be cast before the unclean, you should be in the state of grace. Preferably, you should make a general confession before your marriage, one in which you confess all your past sins so that you will enter your new way of life with a clean slate.

Secondly, you should arrange to have a Nuptial Mass. This Mass, which calls down upon you the greatest of the blessings of the Church, is the means by which you can obtain graces to enable you to meet the unforeseen trials and tribulations which may arise during your future life together. The Nuptial Mass is a fitting accompaniment to the sacrament of Marriage, because just as a Mass is the offering of Christ to God, so too is marriage the offering of the couple to Christ. Both are sacrifices which are pleasing in the sight of God.

And because your marriage is primarily a religious ceremony, it should be planned and celebrated in a religious setting. A king would not be greeted with songs that offended his ears, nor with entertainment that offended his eyes. Nor should profane music, sacrilegious entertainment, and other unseemly things become part of the marriage ceremony. They are out of place.

If you knew a king were calling upon you, you would spend time learning exactly what you should do to entertain him correctly. To prepare yourself properly for marriage, you should attend pre-Cana conferences, if they are held in your diocese. These conferences generally consist of discussions by a priest, doctor, and experienced married couples. They try to answer any questions about marriage you may have. You will also want to read a book or two that will give you an idea of the spiritual, physical and emotional experiences which will lie ahead.

Would you casually call up the President and invite him over to dinner tonight? Hardly. Rather, you would want ample time to prepare. So don't rush into marriage, either.

Allow several months to make all arrangements at the Church. The pastor will need that much time to read the banns of marriage on the three Sundays before the wedding. (These banns are read so that parishioners may make known any impediments which would prevent you from making a valid marriage.) Your Nuptial Mass may take months to schedule.

You will also need time to establish that you are a Catholic, that you are familiar with the basic teachings of the Church, and that you are free to marry. You will have to submit a recent baptismal certificate, as well as a certificate of your First Communion and Confirmation. These certificates can be obtained where the sacraments were performed, and it may take some time to obtain them.

17. THE VOCATION TO THE SINGLE LIFE

At the beginning of our discussion thousands of words ago, we concluded that the main reason for dating is to prepare yourself for marriage. It is fairly obvious that if you do not date, you will not marry, and that you should look upon dating as a possible preparatory step toward marriage.

But I would not want to leave you with the thought that marriage is the only worthwhile vocation for you to aspire to. You know, of course, that the religious life as a priest, brother or nun is a vocation you should also consider with the utmost seriousness. For in serving God as a religious, you would be doing a most noble work and also providing yourself with the best possible assurance that you would achieve your main objective in life—the salvation of your soul.

Priests, religious brothers and nuns you have known were once ordinary youngsters like yourself—youngsters who may have done some dating in their teen years, but who heard God's call somewhere along the line and decided to devote themselves to a life of poverty, chastity and obedience.

Youngsters sometimes think that sirens must sound and lightning must flash to give the signal that they have a vocation to the religious life. It doesn't happen like that at all. Instead, the call generally is heard by people who are seriously considering what they can do to achieve the purpose for which God created them. Nor do you have to be born on your knees with your hands in a praying position to know that God has a special work He wants you to do. If you have good health, the ability to work hard and withstand hardships, you know that you are physically equipped. Although priests, teaching nuns and teaching brothers all have better minds than the average, many communities of religious have places for brothers and sisters who work with their hands while singing the glories of God. They serve in hospitals, for example, or as assistants to missionaries in the field.

Naturally, you also should be reasonably pious, with a reverence for Almighty God, His Church and His ministers. But it is a mistake to think that you must be praying all the time in order to qualify for admission to a religious order.

Important qualities of personality are required for a religious. One is a sense of humility—a realization that you are but an humble creature of God, doing the work of serving other creatures. You need a sense of obedience—a willingness to do what your superiors request of you. And you need a determination to improve yourself, with confidence that God will help you improve your defects if you ask Him to. Of course, you also need the qualities of will to resist temptation —the ability to turn away from that which is temporary or alluring and to keep your mind on the main things of life, the determination to make little sacrifices now to achieve a greater good later.

As you can see, these are qualities which many youngsters possess. The priest in your parish, the missionary, the religious brother, the sister who teaches in grade school—all were youngsters with qualifications like these when they entered training for their vocation. The "stuff they're made of" is little different from that of the stuff of most boys and girls you probably find in your own classroom. But all of them asked God to tell them what to do in their lives and were ready to welcome His call when they heard it.

While the religious makes many sacrifices in his life, it's a serious error to think that he or she doesn't have any compensation. Never underestimate the serenity that comes to an individual who is doing God's work and living in an atmosphere close to the sacraments and the sources of grace. St. Bernard said that the person who leads a religious life "lives more purely, falls more rarely, rises more swiftly, proceeds more carefully, is plentifully blest with grace, lives in greater peace, dies a happier death, is sooner purged from guilt, and finally receives a more glorious reward." You can't beat that!

The satisfactions on this earth are also great. For no matter where his work places him, the religious is devoted to the welfare of his fellowman. He has the satisfaction that comes from helping another human being to achieve his salvation—and the satisfaction of knowing that he is doing the most important work on earth.

You Don't Have *to Marry*

Many persons outside the religious life also have been called to lead a single life. Very often, these are people who can do God's work on earth and save their souls just as well as those who marry.

The point I want to get across is that most people do not *have* to marry in order to lead a successful life. Looking back on some husbands and wives who have brought children into the world, I would say that they would have been better off if they had never taken the marriage vows. In fact, every time you hear or read about a divorce case or a separation, you might be justified in thinking that the people involved should have chosen to remain unmarried.

Our Lord Himself pointed out that the single life can be a sacred one, provided of course that it does not become a cause of sin. Histories of the saints prove this is so.

There may be many reasons for staying single. The best reason of all, of course, is your own decision that it would be easier for you to save your soul in this state than in any other. Perhaps your health would make it more desirable for you to follow the vocation of the single life rather than enter the religious life or marry. Perhaps you will want to care for your parents in their old age.

Or perhaps you will never meet anyone you would want to marry. This reason is as valid as any other, because people who think that they must marry anyone, just for the sake of marrying, will wind up singing a different tune after a while.

You can achieve a great deal with your life as a single person. Recently, for example, there has been a greater recognition of our Christian obligation to help less-developed nations improve their living standards. What a wonderful ambition for a young man or woman to devote a life of helping the peoples of Africa, Asia or Latin America to educate themselves, to eradicate disease and develop more sanitary habits, and to raise their unbelievably low living standards. Often such work can be done best by single persons without family responsibilities.

I know of one young man who went into South America. Working with the local priest, he is doing a great deal to teach the natives how to improve their farming techniques. These natives are still using methods that were in common practice even before the time of Our Lord. They know little or nothing about such things as soil conservation, crop rotation or the use of fertilizers to increase productivity. But with this young man's aid, they are getting bigger and better crops from their land, dramatically increasing the amount of money they get from their labors and therefore greatly improving their standards of living. In many instances, they can now afford to educate their children. They are no longer doomed to lives of utter wretched poverty.

Single persons also can perform many wonderful services without leaving home. They can help as teachers or as nurses' aides in hospitals. They can work to eradicate juvenile delinquency or to bring a little sunshine into the lives of neglected old people and the bedridden. Such persons can lead lives which provide tremendous satisfaction, because they know that they are using their talents to the greatest possible extent.

It's Your Decision

One more point about choosing your vocation. Remember that it's your life—no one else's—and that you're the one who'll have to lead it. This point is especially important to remember if you think you have a call to the religious life or to the single state. Many people have the wrong idea today that everybody should be married. As a result, the person who decides that a way of life other than marriage is not his or her cup of tea, sometimes gets put under a great deal of pressure.

Young men and women who prayerfully decide that they have a religious vocation sometimes are subject to the most absurd experiences. For example, they're asked why they're going to waste their lives—quite a question, incidentally, to ask someone planning to serve God in helping people to save their souls. There's talk that a life of celibacy is difficult. That obedience to a superior is degrading (as though everybody in the outside world can go to work and knock off when he pleases, deciding exactly what work he'll do without having a boss over him). That too much is given up by those who take the vow of poverty (as though the real pleasure of life consisted in riding around in a high-powered automobile or sleeping on silk bed sheets). Sad to say, parents sometimes are the worst offenders in this regard. Some will do all they can to talk their children out of a religious life.

Of course, you should listen to the advice of your elders, but you have an obligation to make up your own mind. You should not undertake any vocation which you yourself don't think you are fitted for. That goes for marriage, the religious life, and the single life as well.

The questions you alone will have to answer are: Which is the work God wants me to do? In what vocation will I have the best chance of saving my soul so that I can look forward with confidence to an eternal reward at the end of my days?

And these questions, remember, get at the main reason why all of us were born. Whether you marry, enter the religious life, or stay single, your life will be a success *only* if at the end of it, you are greeted by Our Father as a faithful servant who performed the work He asked you to do.